Terrestrial Vegetation and Soils Monitoring in the Rincon Mountain District, Saguaro National Park, 2008–2010

Natural Resource Technical Report NPS/SODN/NRDS—2011/216

I0415760

Authors

J. Andrew Hubbard
Sarah E. Studd
Sonoran Desert Network
National Park Service
7660 E. Broadway Blvd., #303
Tucson, AZ 85710

Cheryl L. McIntyre
New Mexico State University
Water Resources Research Institute
MSC 3167
PO Box 30001
Las Cruces, NM 88003

Editing and Design

Alice Wondrak Biel
Sonoran Desert Network
National Park Service
7660 F Broadway Blvd., #303
Tucson, AZ 85710

December 2011

U.S. Department of the Interior
National Park Service
Natural Resource Stewardship and Science
Fort Collins, Colorado

The National Park Service, Natural Resource Stewardship and Science office in Fort Collins, Colorado publishes a range of reports that address natural resource topics of interest and applicability to a broad audience in the National Park Service and others in natural resource management, including scientists, conservation and environmental constituencies, and the public.

The Natural Resource Data Series is intended for timely release of basic data sets and data summaries. Care has been taken to assure accuracy of raw data values, but a thorough analysis and interpretation of the data has not been completed. Consequently, the initial analyses of data in this report are provisional and subject to change.

All manuscripts in the series receive the appropriate level of peer review to ensure that the information is scientifically credible, technically accurate, appropriately written for the intended audience, and designed and published in a professional manner. This report received informal peer review by subject-matter experts who were not directly involved in the collection, analysis, or reporting of the data.

Views, statements, findings, conclusions, recommendations, and data in this report do not necessarily reflect views and policies of the National Park Service, U.S. Department of the Interior. Mention of trade names or commercial products does not constitute endorsement or recommendation for use by the U.S. Government.

This report is available from the Sonoran Desert Network website, http://www.nature.nps.gov/im/units/sodn/, as well as at the Natural Resource Publications Management web site, http://www.nature.nps.gov/publications/nrpm/.

Please cite this publication as:

Hubbard, J. A., S. E. Studd, and C. L. McIntyre. 2011. Terrestrial vegetation and soils monitoring in the Rincon Mountain District, Saguaro National Park, 2008–2010. Natural Resource Data Series NPS/SODN/NRDS—2011/216. National Park Service, Fort Collins, Colorado.

NPS 151/111803, December 2011

Contents

Figures

Tables

Executive Summary

This report summarizes data of the Sonoran Desert Network's first three seasons of terrestrial vegetation and soils monitoring in upland areas of the Rincon Mountain District, Saguaro National Park, in southern Arizona. Thirty-nine permanent monitoring sites were sampled, with another 24 planned for 2011–2012, after which time a detailed status and trend report will be produced. The current report summarizes effort to date, evaluates the sampling design in the context of our monitoring objectives, and suggests modifications to the design.

Based on estimates from this initial data, the sampling design does an excellent job of providing statistical power to detect trends in perennial species, plant lifeforms, and soil stability. The design also provides good power for detecting changes in lifeform composition and soil surface cover, although our projected power for a few variables failed to meet our initial design criteria. Species detectability appears to be very reasonable based on species-accumulation curves. Although only about 29% of the known park flora has been detected to date, the protocol does not call for differentiating annuals to species (with the exception of exotic plants), nor are we sampling aquatic, riparian, or xeroriparian systems as part of this protocol.

The elevation × soil texture stratification scheme appears to be effective, although vegetation community similarity of the two rocky strata at lower-elevation sites (<4,500') did not differ significantly. This is likely a real ecological similarity, as we explicitly addressed the possibility of statistical artifacts (i.e, from the small sample sizes to date) in our 2010 sampling. It is likely that these strata will be combined in the final 2012 analyses. We will readdress this question in the 2011 data summary.

Overall, we conclude that the sampling and response designs are efficient and effective, and should provide data that meet our monitoring objectives. We will continue to evaluate and adjust our sampling strategy annually, culminating in the full analysis for the comprehensive status and trends reports after the 2012 season. Therefore, it is important that results in this and other annual data summaries not be directly interpreted for evaluating the condition of park resources.

Acronyms

ANOSIM	analysis of similarity
AVG	average
GRTS	Generalized Random Tessellation Stratified
MDC	minimum detectable change
MDS	non-metric multidimensional scaling
n	number
NP	national park
NPS	National Park Service
RMD	Rincon Mountain District
RRQRR	Reversed Randomized Quadrant Recursive Raster
SD	standard deviation
Sdiff	standard deviation of the differences
SE	standard error
SODN	Sonoran Desert Network

Acknowledgements

We thank Superintendent Darla Sidles and the staff and volunteers of Saguaro NP for their on-site support of the field effort and the Sonoran Desert Network (SODN) Inventory and Monitoring Program. Beth Fallon, Laura Crumbacher, Aedan Berge, Kate Connor, Betsy Vance, Laura Tennant, and Steve Buckley conducted the field-data collection, often under arduous (but always scenic) conditions. Expert data processing and management was completed by SODN Data Manager Kristen Beaupré, and Laura Crumbacher updated the master plant lists.

1 Introduction

1.1 Background

Generating more than 99.9% of Earth's biomass (Whittaker 1975), plants are the primary producers of life on our planet. Vegetation therefore represents much of the biological foundation of terrestrial ecosystems, and it comprises or interacts with all primary structural and functional components of these systems. Vegetation dynamics can indicate the integrity of ecological processes, productivity trends, and ecosystem interactions that can otherwise be difficult to monitor. Land management actions often focus on manipulating vegetation to achieve park management objectives, with defined conditions based on community structure or lifeform composition.

In the Sonoran Desert ecoregion (Bailey 1998), vegetation composition, distribution, and production are highly influenced by edaphic factors, such as soil texture, mineralogy depth, and landform type (McAuliffe 1999). Especially as they relate to water, these influences are magnified at local scales, as described by pioneering desert ecologist Forrest Shreve:

> The profound influence of soil upon desert vegetation is to be attributed to its strong control of the amount, availability and continuity of water supply. This fundamental requisite in plants is the most effective single factor in the differentiation of desert communities (Shreve 1951).

As such, a fundamental understanding of soils and landforms is essential for evaluating vegetation patterns and processes (McAuliffe 1999).

The Sonoran Desert Network (SODN), as part of the National Park Service's Inventory and Monitoring (I&M) Program, has identified terrestrial vegetation and dynamic soil functional attributes as important ecosystem monitoring parameters or "vital signs" (NPS 2005) that provide key insights into the integrity of terrestrial ecosystems at Saguaro National Park (NP; Figure 1-1). Indicators of terrestrial vegetation integrity include vegetation community structure, lifeform abundance, status and trends of established exotic plants, and early detection of previously undetected exotic plants. Indicators of soil dynamic function and erosion resistance include the cover of mineral soil and the stability of surface soil aggregates.

1.2 Goals and objectives

The overall goal of the SODN terrestrial vegetation and soils monitoring program is to ascertain broad-scale changes in vegetation and dynamic soils properties in the context of changes in other ecological drivers, stressors, processes, and focal resources of interest. This integrated approach explores patterns and identifies candidate explanations to support effective management and protection of park natural resources in a cumulative fashion, such that the results of each successive round of monitoring builds upon the knowledge gained from previous efforts and related research and monitoring activities.

Specific, measurable objectives for SODN terrestrial vegetation and soils monitoring (Hubbard et al. in review) at Saguaro NP are to determine the status of and detect trends in (over five-year intervals):

1. Terrestrial *vegetation cover* for common (≥10% absolute canopy cover) perennial species, including non-native plants, and all plant lifeforms.

2. Terrestrial *vegetation frequency* of uncommon (<10% absolute canopy cover) perennial species, including non-native plants.

3. Terrestrial *soil cover* by substrate classes (bare soil, litter, vegetation, biological soil crust, rock fragments of several size classes) that influence resistance to erosion.

4. Terrestrial *soil stability* of surface aggregates by stability class (1–6).

5. Basal *cover and frequency of biological soil crusts* by lichen growth form and morphological group.

1.3 Scope of this report

This document summarizes the results of the first three years of terrestrial vegetation and soils monitoring in the Rincon Mountain District of Saguaro NP. As Saguaro NP is the second-largest unit in the Sonoran Desert Network, we employ a multi-year sampling strategy in which one-fifth of the monitoring sites are sampled in a given year, with the entire complement completed after five field seasons (i.e., in 2012). Because only three-fifths of the sampling has occurred to date, and we do not synthesize and interpret the current information in the context of status or trends. Instead, the objectives of this report are to:

- Document the processed data from the first three years of this multi-year effort.

- Evaluate the stratification approach and sample sizes based on vegetation similarity, estimated statistical power, and species detectability.

- If warranted by the data, adjust strata and sample sizes to ensure we are meeting the monitoring objectives.

It is therefore critical that the reader not draw overall conclusions based on this report alone.

We will continue to produce annual data summaries and refine the sampling design as necessary, with a much more detailed and comprehensive synthesis report to be created after the final complement of sampling in 2012. For an example of a final status and trend report, see Terrestrial Vegetation and Soils Monitoring at Fort Bowie National Historic Site: 2008 Status Report (Hubbard et al. 2010), available at http://science.nature.nps.gov/im/units/sodn/docs/AR_FOBO_Uplands_2009.pdf .

We address the Tucson Mountain District of Saguaro NP as a separate unit, reflecting the disconnected nature and substantial inherent ecological differences between the two units. The thematic scope of this report is limited to terrestrial ecosystems. Aquatic resources, including riparian and xeroriparian vegetation, are addressed in SODN protocols for monitoring Washes and Seeps, Springs, and Tinajas.

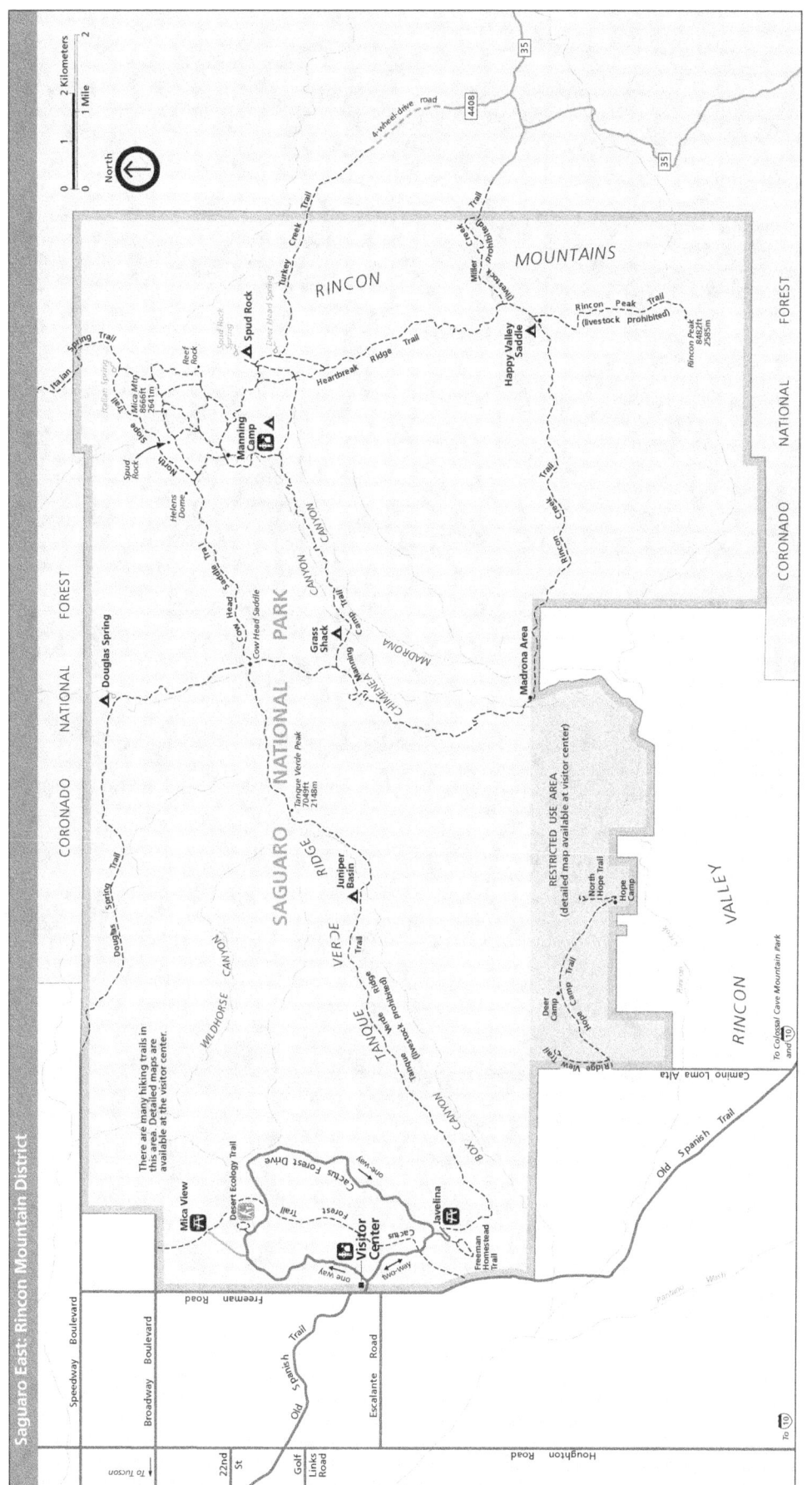

Figure 1-1. Rincon Mountain District, Saguaro National Park.

2 Methods

2.1 Response design

The response design for this protocol employs permanent, 20 × 50-m sampling plots (Figure 2-1). The 50-m edges of the plot run parallel with the contours of the site. Vegetation sampling is performed, in conjunction with soil cover and stability measures, along six transects within each plot. In the spaces between transects (subplots), within-plot frequency is estimated by noting the occurrence of any plant species or lifeform not observed on the adjacent transects. See Hubbard and others (in review) for details on plot configuration and data collection.

2.1.1 Vegetation, soil cover, and biological soil crusts: Line-point intercept

Line-point intercept is a common and efficient technique for measuring the vegetation cover of plants. Line-point intercept measures the number of "hits" of a given species out of the total number of points measured (Elzinga et al. 1998; Bonham 1989). Vegetation was recorded within three height categories along each of the six transects using the line-point intercept method, with points spaced every 0.5 m (240 points total). The three height categories were field (<0.5 m), subcanopy (0.5–2.0 m), and canopy (>2.0 m) (Table 2-1). Perennial vegetation was recorded to species and annual vegetation was recorded to lifeform, with the exception of a suite of annual non-native plants that were recorded to the species level. Soil cover (see Hubbard et al. in review, SOP #5) was recorded by substrate class (e.g., rock, gravel, litter), with biological soil crust cover recorded to morphological group (e.g., light cyanobacteria, dark cyanobacteria, lichen, moss).

Table 2-1. Height categories for vegetation measurement.

Layer	Height
Field	<0.5 m
Subcanopy	0.5–2.0 m
Canopy	>2.0 m

2.1.2 Vegetation frequency: Subplots

The area between any two adjacent transects formed the boundary of 10 × 20-m subplots that were used to estimate within-plot frequency of perennial plant species, exotic plants, and all lifeforms. The occurrence of any species/lifeform not measured on the adjacent line-point transect was recorded to determine a within-plot frequency of 0–5. Figure 2-1 explains the relationship between each subplot and its corresponding adjacent transect.

2.1.3 Soil aggregate stability

Surface soil aggregate stability was measured using a modified wet aggregate stability method (Herrick et al. 2005a). Within each plot, samples were attempted at 48 pre-determined points on either side of the six line-point intercept transects. The uniformly sized (2–3 mm thick and 6–8 mm on each side) samples were tested in groups of 16. Each sample was placed on a screen and soaked in water for five minutes. After five minutes, the samples were slowly dipped up and down in the water, with the remaining amount of soil recorded as an index of the wet aggregate stability of the sample. Samples were scored from 1 to 6, with 6 being the most stable.

2.1.4 Biological soil crust cover and frequency: Point-quadrats

In addition to line-point intercept measurements, biological soil crust cover was measured using 0.25-m² quadrats. Three quadrats were measured per transect using the point-quadrat method (similar in concept to line-point intercept), with 16 intercept measurements per quadrat, resulting in 18 quadrats and 288 measurements per plot. At each intercept, biological soil crusts were recorded as light cyanobacteria, dark cyanobacteria, bryophytes (moss and liverworts), or lichens by growth form. The observer then visually surveyed the quadrat for any lichen growth form or morphological group that was present. Soil-crust frequency by lichen growth form and morphological group was determined by the number of quadrats occupied relative to the total number of quadrats (i.e., 18). The SODN terrestrial vegetation and soils monitoring protocol (Hubbard et al. in review, SOP #6) provides a detailed description of the point-quadrat methodology. The initial round of sampling at Saguaro NP will help SODN to determine differences between the line-point intercept and point-quadrat methodologies.

2.1.5 Soil and site characterization

Proximate soil and landform factors are known to influence vegetation and dynamic soil

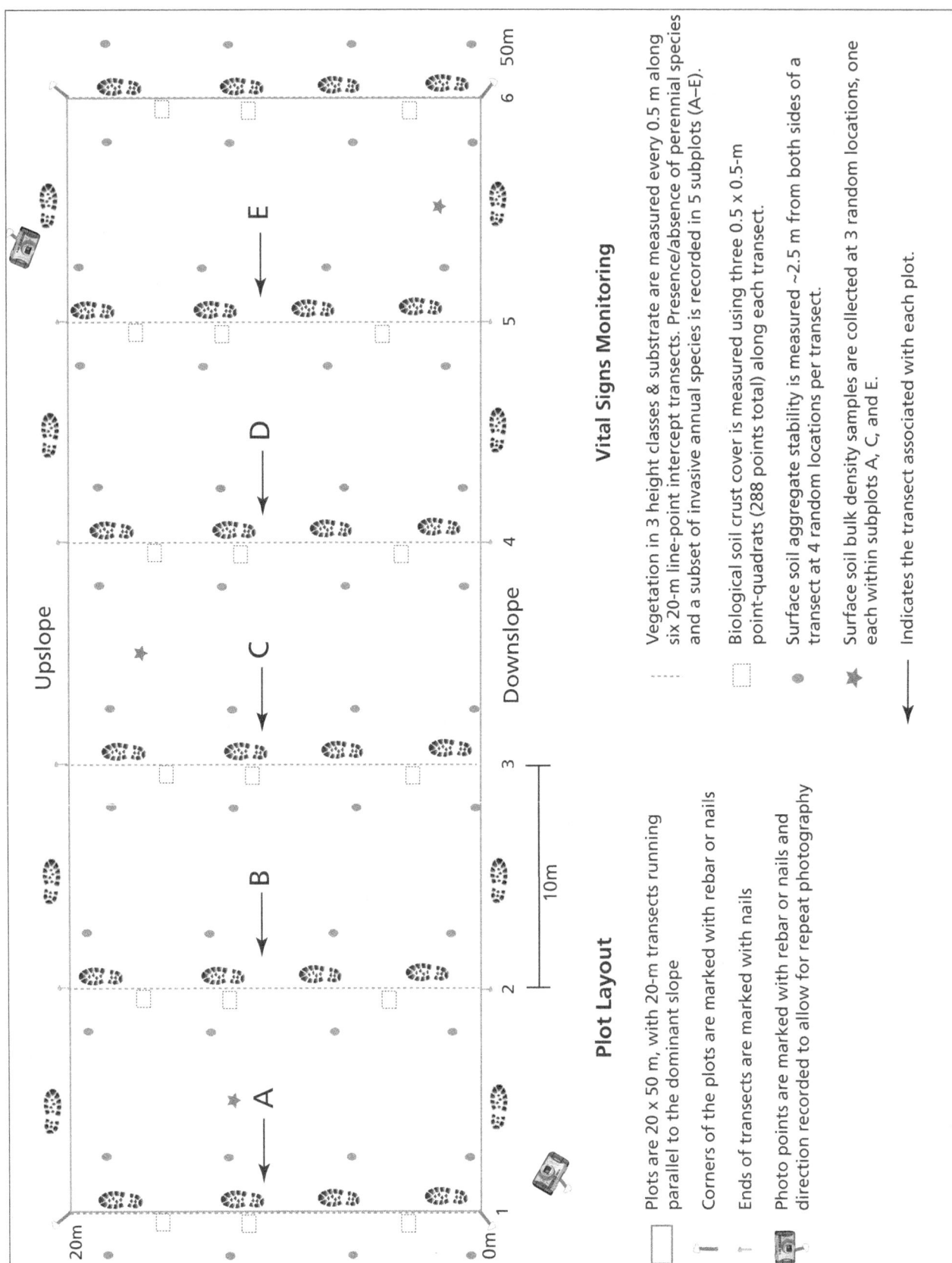

Plot Layout

— Plots are 20 x 50 m, with 20-m transects running parallel to the dominant slope

□ Corners of the plots are marked with rebar or nails

— Ends of transects are marked with nails

📷 Photo points are marked with rebar or nails and direction recorded to allow for repeat photography

Vital Signs Monitoring

— Vegetation in 3 height classes & substrate are measured every 0.5 m along six 20-m line-point intercept transects. Presence/absence of perennial species and a subset of invasive annual species is recorded in 5 subplots (A–E).

□ Biological soil crust cover is measured using three 0.5 x 0.5-m point-quadrats (288 points total) along each transect.

● Surface soil aggregate stability is measured ~2.5 m from both sides of a transect at 4 random locations per transect.

★ Surface soil bulk density samples are collected at 3 random locations, one each within subplots A, C, and E.

→ Indicates the transect associated with each plot.

Figure 2-1. Terrestrial vegetation and soils monitoring plot design. See Hubbard et al. (in review) for additional details on design and data collection.

function parameters at local scales (McAuliffe 1999). To characterize the soil and landscape attributes of each plot, a suite of topoedaphic variables was collected through site diagrams, repeat photo points, and collection of soil cores. Landform, slope position, and parent material were recorded at each plot. Slope measurements (%) and descriptions (type and position) were used to depict surface-flow patterns of the hillslope within each plot. Permanent photo points were established at each plot corner to characterize general site physiognomy and as an aid to interpreting quantitative trend data in successive sampling periods. In addition, general site descriptions (including observed disturbances, such as fire) were collected for each plot.

2.2 Sampling design

2.2.1 Overview

We allocated a total of 63 permanent monitoring plots in a spatially balanced arrangement (see Section 2.2.3), based on and preliminary data analysis and a priori expectations of required sample size to meet our criteria for statistical power and detectability (see Sections 2.2.5–2.2.6). Terrestrial vegetation and soils plots were proportionately allocated to five strata based on elevation and soil type (Table 2-2, Figure 2-2). Stratification (see Section 3.2.2, Hubbard et al. in review) was employed to reduce spatial variability and increase sampling efficiency.

Access is a prime concern at the unit. We used a cost-surface approach (Figure 2-3), based on modeled travel time, to adjust inclusion probabilities for sampling plots. Appendix A of the monitoring protocol (Hubbard et al. in review) pro-

vides the details; essentially, plot locations were weighted toward sites that were more accessible, although all locations had a chance of being selected (except those excluded due to safety concerns or possible harm to resources; see Section 2.2.4). Consequently, inference from the plots at Saguaro NP is to all terrestrial areas of the unit by elevation × soil strata, excepting the areas discussed in Section 2.2.4 below.

2.2.2 Annual sampling

Permanent plots are employed to increase our ability to efficiently detect trends, by explicitly partitioning spatial and temporal variability (Elzinga et al. 1998). As with all designs, there are inherent tradeoffs with using permanent plots, as discussed in Hubbard and others (in review). The primary disadvantage at larger units (such as the Rincon Mountain District; RMD) is that sampling across landscapes (space) is reduced as field effort is dedicated to revisiting existing plots.

To ensure adequate spatial coverage, we employ a simple rotating panel design (McDonald 2003) that allocates plots annually, such that each plot is revisited every five years [1,4], in line with our assumptions regarding the timing of biologically meaningful change (Hubbard et al. in review). Using this approach, the total population of plots in a park is apportioned evenly per year. For the RMD, the total anticipated sample size is 60 plots; ideally, with 12 plots sampled each year (Table 2-3). However, site suitability and logistical constraints affect actual sampling effort each year.

The advantages of this design are that (1) the influence of interannual variation (i.e., noise) is less pronounced for the analysis of five-year

Table 2-2. Allocation of permanent terrestrial vegetation and soils monitoring plots by strata, Rincon Mountain District, Saguaro NP.

Stratum	Elevation	% rock fragments	Total area (acres)	Percentage of total		Plots per stratum	
				Park area	Frame area	Number	Number per year
Excluded			18,372	27	0	0	0
201	<3,700'	>35%	1,455	2	3	5	1 or 0
202	<3,700'	35–90%	9,045	13	19	11	2 or 3
302	3,701–4,500'	35–90%	6,575	10	13	8	1 or 2
402	4,501–6,000'	35–90%	16,719	25	34	21	4 or 5
502	>6,001'	35–90%	14,952	22	31	18	3 or 4

Strata with <5% of park area are generally excluded. However, we included the 201 stratum, which contains the "Cactus Forest" area, a prime management zone at Saguaro NP.

Vegetation & Soils Monitoring Plots

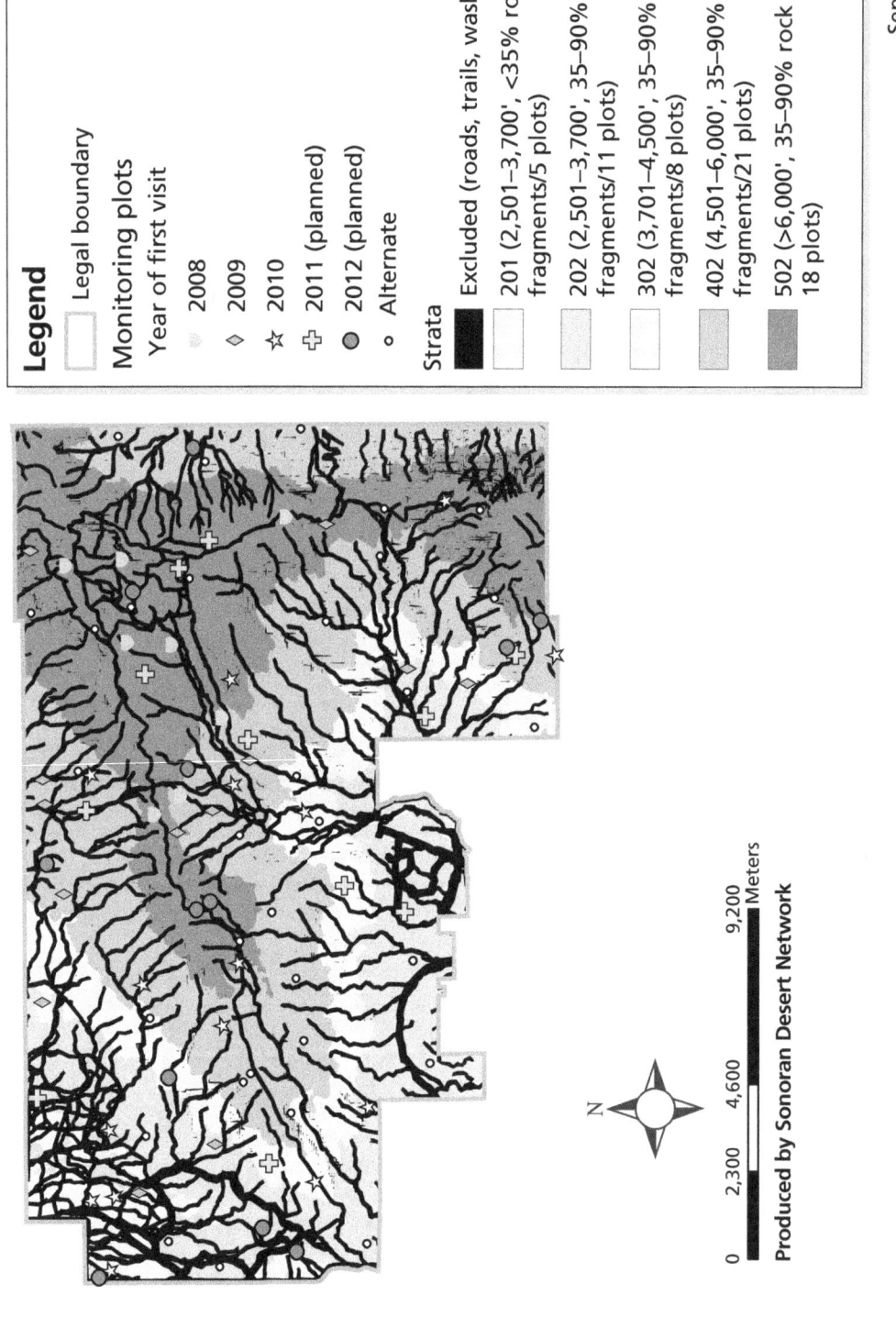

Legend

Legal boundary

Monitoring plots
Year of first visit

- 2008
- 2009
- 2010
- 2011 (planned)
- 2012 (planned)
- Alternate

Strata

- Excluded (roads, trails, washes/0 plots)
- 201 (2,501–3,700', <35% rock fragments/5 plots)
- 202 (2,501–3,700', 35–90% rock fragments/11 plots)
- 302 (3,701–4,500', 35–90% rock fragments/8 plots)
- 402 (4,501–6,000', 35–90% rock fragments/21 plots)
- 502 (>6,000', 35–90% rock fragments/18 plots)

September 2011

0   2,300   4,600   9,200
                                   Meters

N

Produced by Sonoran Desert Network

Figure 2-2. Distribution of terrestrial vegetation and soils monitoring plots at the Rincon Mountain District, Saguaro NP.

Vegetation & Soils Monitoring Plots

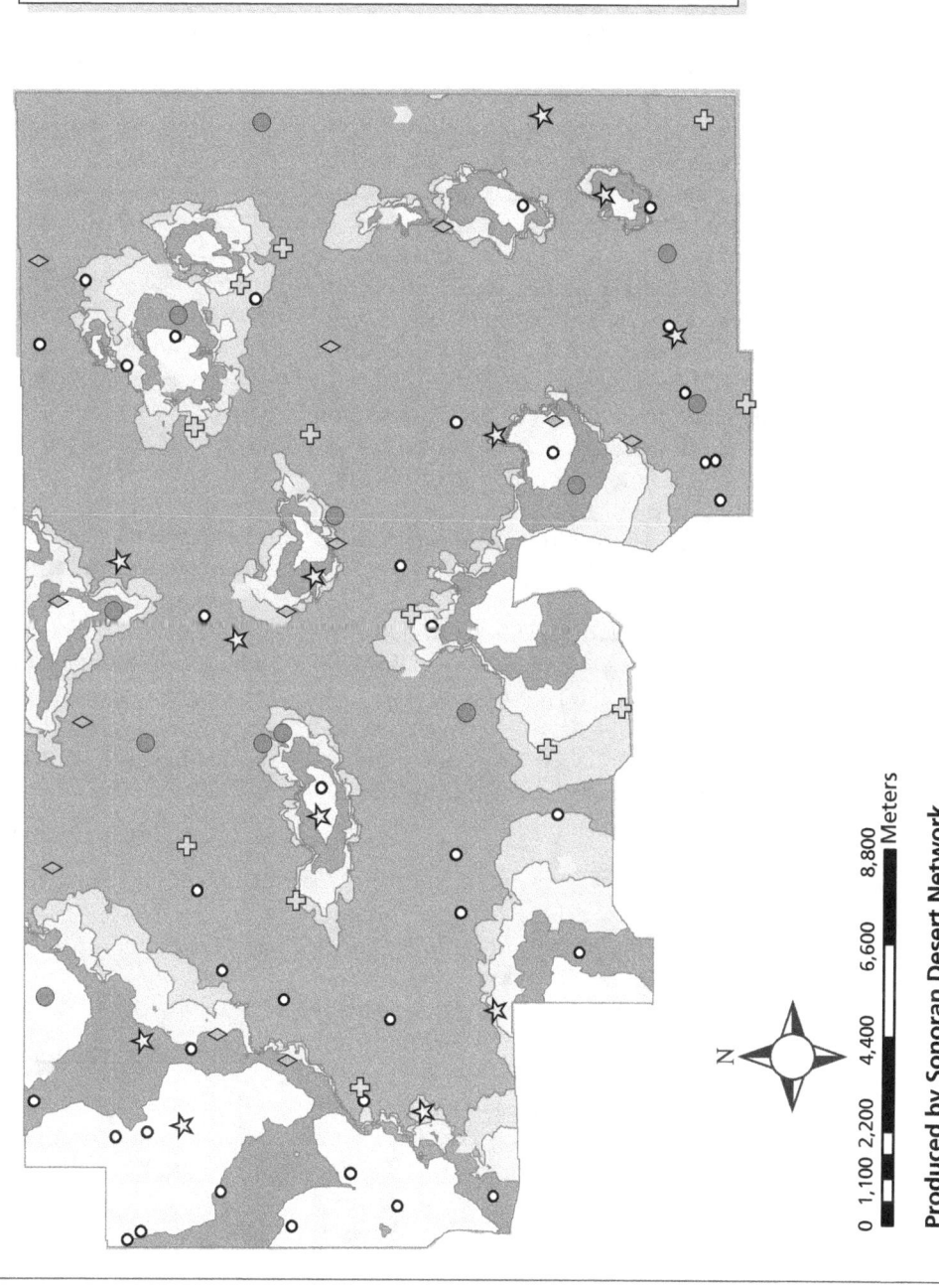

Legend

Park boundary

Monitoring plots
Year of first visit

- 2008
- 2009
- 2010
- 2011 (planned)
- 2012 (planned)
- Alternate

Hiking time

- <0.5 hr
- 0.5–1 hr
- 1–1.5 hrs
- 1.5–2 hrs
- >2 hrs

December 2008

N

0 1,100 2,200   4,400   6,600   8,800
Meters

Produced by Sonoran Desert Network

Figure 2-3. Modeled travel time relative to terrestrial vegetation and soil plot locations, Rincon Mountain District, Saguaro NP. Travel time was used to create a cost surface that weighted plot selection towards more accessible sites.

Table 2-3. Sampling schedule for Rincon Mountain District, Saguaro NP.

Strata	Plots sampled			Plots not yet sampled	
	2008	2009	2010	2011	2012
201 (non-rocky soils, <3,700')	2, 3		4, 5, 6		
202 (rocky soils, <3,700')	3	4, 5	6, 7	8, 9, 10	11, 12, 13
302 (rocky soils, 3,701–4,500')	1	4, 7	12, 13	14, 15	16
402 (rocky soils, 4,501–6,000')	1, 3	2, 5, 6, 7, 8	10, 12, 13, 15, 16	17, 18, 19, 20, 21	22, 23, 24, 25
502 (rocky soils, >6,001')	1, 2, 3, 6, 26, 27	5, 7, 8	9, 10, 11	12, 13, 14	15, 16, 17

Values are the site labels within each stratum. Adjustments within and between strata may occur based on early results, and individual plots may be rejected due to sampling and safety criteria. Section 2.2.2 describes the stratification scheme.

trends; and (2) there are tremendous efficiency gains, from the perspective of fielding and funding sampling crews, as effort is spread evenly over five-year intervals. The disadvantages are that (1) the effects of individual stochastic events may be difficult to evaluate (Hubbard et al. in review) and (2) detecting trends requires at least 10 years of data collection (i.e., two sampling intervals for all plots). Rotating-panel designs generally allow trend detection over shorter time periods (particularly when a subset of the plots is monitored continually), but sampling intensity is unlikely to meet our statistical-power and species-detection goals (see Sections 2.2.5–2.2.6). We ruled out intensive annual monitoring of a subset of plots due to concerns over plot degradation, as discussed in the SODN natural and cultural resource compliance effort (NPS 2005b).

If a major disturbance (e.g., fire, extended periods of temperature extremes, mass soil movement) occurs in the intervening years, we may collect additional plot data to characterize and account for the potential effects of these important stochastic events.

2.2.3 Spatial balance

The spatial sampling design for this protocol employs permanent, 20 × 50-m sampling plots, allocated through a Reversed Randomized Quadrant-Recursive Raster (RRQRR) spatially balanced design (Theobald et al. 2007), using the "spatially balanced sample" function in the STARMAP Spatial Sampling Toolbox in ArcGIS 9.0 (http://www.spatialecology.com/htools/index.php). This tool produces a design that is spatially well-balanced, probability-based, flexible, and simple (Theobald et al. 2007). Because it tries

to maximize the spatial independence between plots, the spatially balanced sampling design should provide more information per plot, thus increasing efficiency (Theobald et al. 2007).

Spatially balanced designs, such as RRQRR and the Generalized Random Tessellation Stratified (GRTS) approach (Stevens and Olsen 2004), are increasingly being applied to ecosystem monitoring (e.g., Environmental Protection Agency Ecological Monitoring and Assessment Program) because they provide the advantages of a probabilistic design (Stehman 1999) and ensure spatial balance regardless of overall sample size. RRQRR designs facilitate adding or removing sites in a spatially balanced manner if statistical power, financial considerations, or additional monitoring objectives warrant adjusting the sample size. This scaling ability is an important advantage, as (1) the number of plots per park cannot always be adequately estimated a priori (see Section 3.4.2, Hubbard et al. in review) and (2) future changes in technology, objectives, and budgets may necessitate increasing or decreasing sample sizes.

2.2.4 Sampling frame

The sampling frame for the RMD (see Figure 2-2) includes all terrestrial areas within unit boundaries, except for the following:

• Slopes of ≥ 45° (for crew safety)

• Roads and buildings (including 100-m buffer)

• Trails, washes, and streams (including 50-m buffer)

• Selected fragile cultural features (e.g., Manning Cabin)

The total area excluded under these criteria was 18,372 acres (~7,435 ha), or 27% of the unit area.

2.2.5 Management assessment points as the link between science and management

To achieve the National Park Service's core mission of resource protection, resource management and monitoring must be explicitly linked (Bingham et al. 2007). We advocate the use of management assessment points as a bridge between science and management. Management assessment points are "pre-selected points along a continuum of resource-indicator values where scientists and managers have agreed to stop and assess the status or trend of a resource relative to program goals, natural variation, or potential concerns" (Bennetts et al. 2007).

Management assessment points therefore aid interpretation of ecological information within a management context. They do not define strict management or ecological thresholds, inevitably result in management actions, or reflect any legal or regulatory standard; they are only intended to serve as a potential early warning system allowing scientists and managers to pause, review the available information in detail, and consider options. Bennetts and others (2007) provided a detailed explanation of this concept and its application to monitoring and management of protected areas.

Although no management assessment points have been formally established for Saguaro NP, we intend to develop assessment points relevant to terrestrial vegetation and soils as part of the Natural Resource Condition Assessment (NRCA) process (see http://www.nature.nps.gov/water/NRCondition_Assessment_Program/Index.cfm). We expect the NRCA effort at Saguaro NP to begin in 2012 or 2013, pending funding and approval from the National Park Service Water Resources Division. For an example of the application of management assessment points, see Terrestrial Vegetation and Soils Monitoring at Fort Bowie National Historic Site: 2008 Status Report (Hubbard et al. 2010), available at: http://science.nature.nps.gov/im/units/sodn/docs/AR_FOBO_Uplands_2009.pdf.

2.2.6 Statistical power to distinguish status from management assessment points

Estimating our statistical power to distinguish current conditions (i.e., status) from management assessment points (see previous section) is important for both protocol design (especially for determining adequate sample sizes) and data interpretation. Adequate sample size (number of plots) is estimated by (Herrick et al. 2005b):

$$n = \frac{(S)^2 \, (Z_\alpha + Z_\beta)^2}{(MDC)^2}$$

Where:

- S = standard deviation of the sample,

- Z_α = Z-coefficient for false change (Type I) error (we set at 90%),

- Z_β = Z-coefficient for missed-change (Type II) error (we set at 10%), and

MDC = minimum detectable change size between time 1 and time 2 (set at 5–20%).

Bonham (1989), Elzinga and others (1998), and Herrick and others (2005b) provide detailed discussions of statistical power to detect differences from a standard.

2.2.7 Statistical power to detect trends

Statistical power is also important for evaluating trends (change over time) in monitoring parameters. Adequate sample size (number of plots) for detecting a trend of a given size across a landscape with permanent plots is estimated from:

$$n = \frac{(S_{diff})^2 \, (Z_\alpha + Z_\beta)^2}{(MDC)^2}$$

Where:

- S_{diff} = Standard deviation of the differences between paired samples,

- Z_α = Z-coefficient for false change (Type I) error (we set at 90%),

- Z_β = Z-coefficient for missed-change (Type II) error (we set at 10%), and

- MDC = minimum detectable change size between time 1 and time 2 (set at 5–20%).

Because we only have one sampling interval for this report, we estimated "S_{diff}" using the following equation:

$$S_{diff} = (S_1)(\sqrt{(2(1 - corr_{diff}))})$$

Where:

- S_1 = Sample standard deviation among sampling units at first time period, and

$corr_{diff}$ = estimated correlation coefficient between time 1 and time 2, set at 0.75.

Bonham (1989), Elzinga and others (1998), and Herrick and others (2005b) provide detailed discussions of statistical power to detect trend.

2.2.8 Evaluation of strata

The terrestrial vegetation monitoring design apportions long-term monitoring sites to strata to improve the efficiency of parkwide estimation of monitoring parameters of interest. It is assumed that vegetation and dynamic soil functional attributes respond differently to environmental factors that can be clearly defined and are immutable over management and monitoring timescales (Bonham 1989).

To evaluate the efficiency and pertinence of our preselected elevation strata, we contrasted the similarity of the vegetation communities on each stratum using analysis of similarity (ANOSIM) and non-metric multidimensional scaling, non-parametric, multivariate community analysis techniques that make few assumptions about the data, yielding a simple yet powerful analysis tool (Clarke and Warwick 2001).

3 Results

3.1 Evaluation of strata

Analysis of similarity results (Table 3-1) indicated significant differences ($P \leq 4.0\%$) between plant communities in four strata groupings by elevation and soil type:

- 201 (2,501–3,700', not rocky (i.e., the Cactus Forest area)

- 202 and 302, collectively (2,501–4,500', very to extremely rocky)

- 402 (4,501–6,000', very to extremely rocky)

- 502 (>6,000', very to extremely rocky)

Elevation differences between the 202 and 302 very to extremely rocky sites did not significantly ($P \geq 44\%$) differentiate plant community composition. Aspect does not appear to explain the similarities between the two strata. Non-metric multidimensional scaling (MDS; Figure 3-1) illustrates the similarity of sites by strata. A few plots had virtually no canopy cover, greatly skewing similarity. As a result, MDS was also performed on the subset (n=36) of plots that contained canopy cover (Figure 3-1d). See Appendix A for complete results.

3.2 Plant species detectability

Line-point intercepts on the 39 monitoring sites sampled from 2008 through 2010 detected 228 perennial species, and employing the frequency subplots added 108 perennial species. However, slope decreased markedly on species accumulation curves (Figure 3-2), suggesting diminishing returns for detecting new species with increased sampling intensity.

3.3 Power to detect trends

3.2.1 Plant lifeforms and common perennial species

Our proposed sampling design met or exceeded our expectations for statistical power to detect trends in common perennial species based on our design criteria (i.e., to detect a 10% absolute change in foliar cover with 90% power and 10% chance of a false change error). Our data indicate that we will be able to detect a 5% change (absolute foliar cover) for nearly all detected perennial species with the current level of sampling

Table 3-1. ANOSIM results for contrasting vegetation composition by strata for (a) field, (b) subcanopy, and (c) canopy height classes for terrestrial vegetation monitoring at the Rincon Mountain District, Saguaro NP, 2008–2010.

a. Field (<0.5 m)
Global R: 0.592, P = 0.1%

Groups	R	P
201 vs. 202	0.728	**0.8%**
201 vs. 302	0.836	**0.8%**
201 vs. 402	0.966	**0.1%**
201 vs. 502	0.601	**0.1%**
202 vs. 302	0.004	44.4%
202 vs. 402	0.940	**0.1%**
202 vs. 502	0.614	**0.1%**
302 vs. 402	0.870	**0.1%**
302 vs. 502	0.588	**0.1%**
402 vs. 502	0.284	**0.1%**

b. Subcanopy (0.5–2.0 m)
Global R: 0.726, P = 0.1%

Groups	R	P
201 vs. 202	0.654	**0.8%**
201 vs. 302	0.668	**0.8%**
201 vs. 402	0.987	**0.1%**
201 vs. 502	0.993	**0.2%**
202 vs. 302	-0.110	77.0%
202 vs. 402	0.952	**0.1%**
202 vs. 502	0.942	**0.1%**
302 vs. 402	0.907	**0.1%**
302 vs. 502	0.867	**0.1%**
402 vs. 502	0.314	**0.1%**

c. Canopy (>2.0 m)
Global R: 0.560, P = 0.1%

Groups	R	P
201 vs. 202	0.359	8.9%
201 vs. 302	0.363	**3.2%**
201 vs. 402	0.633	**0.2%**
201 vs. 502	0.954	**0.1%**
202 vs. 302	-0.093	62.9%
202 vs. 402	0.616	**0.2%**
202 vs. 502	0.928	**0.2%**
302 vs. 402	0.646	**0.1%**
302 vs. 502	0.972	**0.1%**
402 vs. 502	0.297	**0.1%**

Bolded values are statistically significant at our selected P value threshold.

a) Field (<0.5 m)

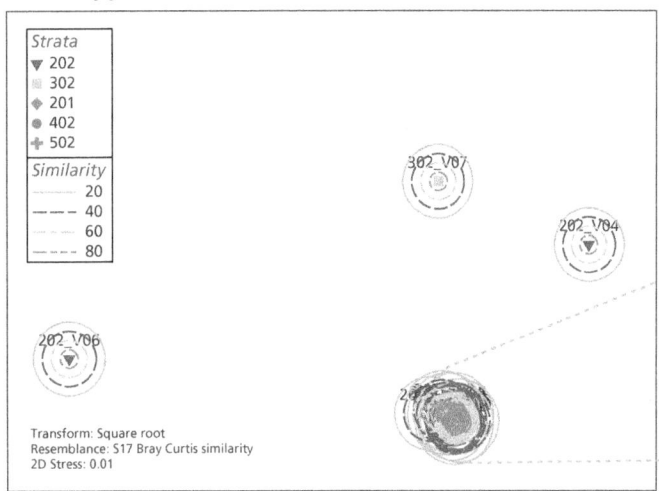

b) Subcanopy (0.5–2.0 m)

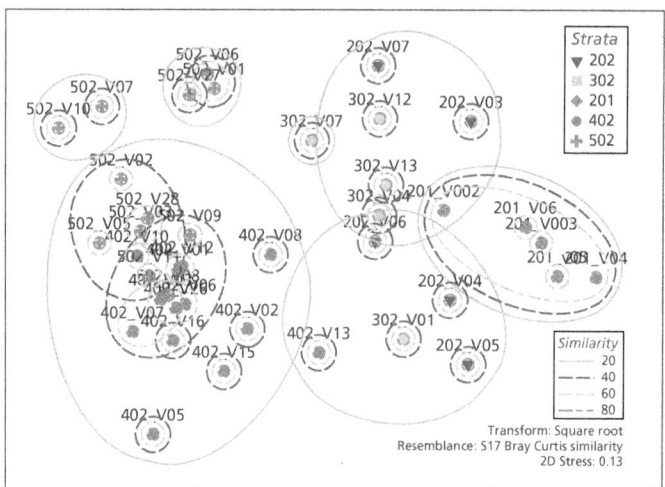

c) Canopy (>2.0 m)

d) Canopy (>2.0 m) subset

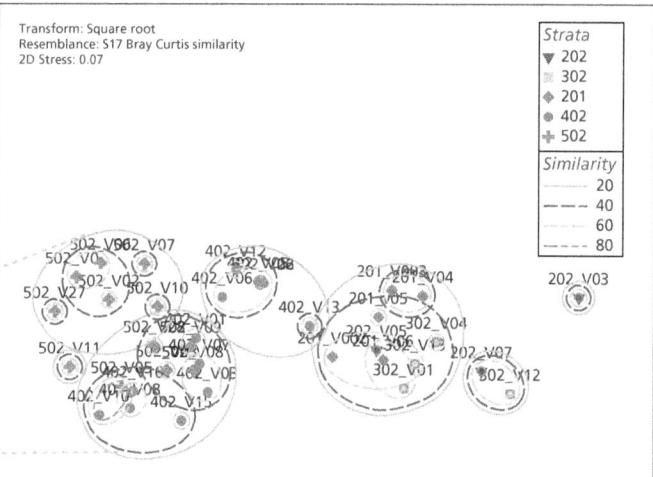

Figure 3-1. MDS analysis indicates similarity of (a) field, (b) subcanopy, and (c) canopy communities. The distance between any two points increases as their composition and structure differ. Figure 3-1d depicts the MDS on the subset of plots (n=36) that contained canopy cover.

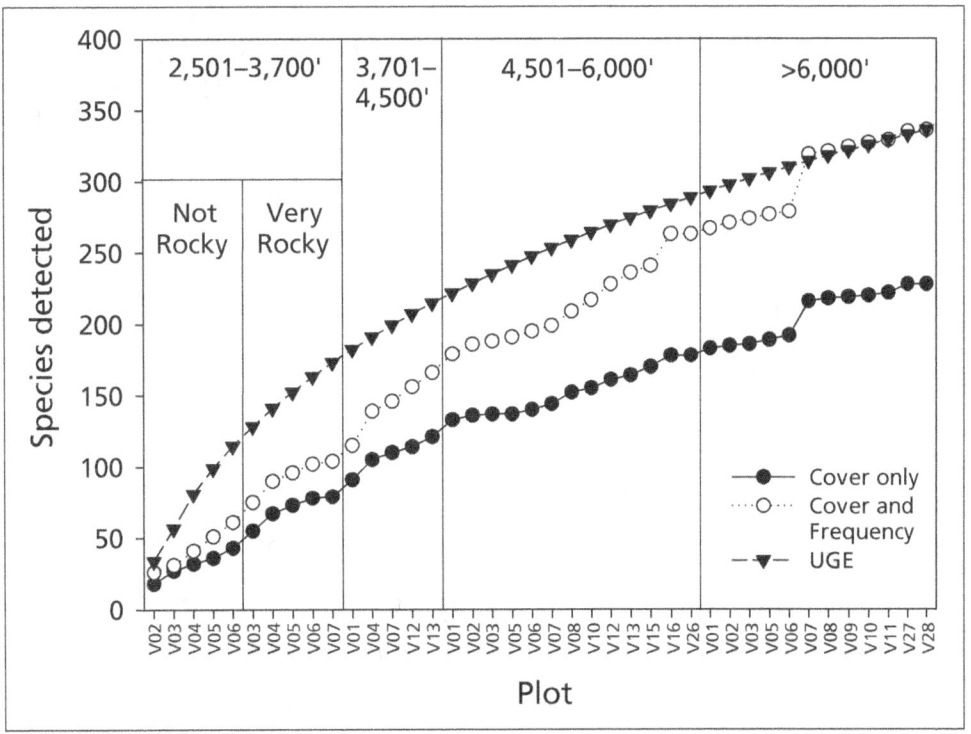

Figure 3-2. Species area curves for cover and frequency data collected on terrestrial vegetation and soils plots at the Rincon Mountain District, Saguaro NP, 2008–2010. Curves show cumulative numbers of species detected as plots are added. UGE = mean species accumulation curve with samples entered in random order (Ugland et al. 2003).

intensity (Appendix A, Tables A1–A3). Plot-level data are given in Appendix A, Tables A1–A3.

Most lifeforms also met or exceeded our criteria, with a few exceptions. Perennial grasses in the field layer on rocky sites in stratum 302 just missed our criteria; we estimate that we will be able to detect an 11% change in foliar cover. Tree lifeforms in the canopies of high-elevation sites (>6,000', 502 stratum) also exceeded our change detection threshold by 1%. As trees comprise much of the vegetative cover of the high-elevation plots, there was a contingent effect on total canopy cover, which also exceeded our criteria by 1%.

3.2.2 Uncommon perennial species

Our design met or exceeded our sampling objectives for detecting trends in most uncommon perennial species (i.e., to detect at least a 10% change in within-plot frequency with 90% power and 10% chance of false change error) for species encountered only in frequency subplots. Four species with relatively high within-plot frequencies and high variance had less power to detect change (Table A4) based on frequency. However, all of these species were also detected as vegetation cov-

er along the line-point transects, which provide far more precise estimates and improved statistical power than frequency (Tables A1–A3). Plot-level data are provided in Appendix B in the electronic version of this document.

3.2.3 Soil parameters

Our design met or exceeded our sampling objectives for soil substrate cover and surface soil aggregate stability class for most soil parameters (i.e., to detect at least a 10% change or 1 stability class, with 90% power and 10% chance of false change error) at the proposed sampling intensity (Table A5). Exceptions were litter + duff cover, and gravel cover on rocky sites below 3,701' (202 stratum); we estimate that we can detect a 13% change in these two substrate parameters for the 202 stratum. Two parameters characterize soil stability: average soil stability class (0–6), both under and away from vegetation cover; and the percentage of samples both under and away from vegetation cover in the most stable category (i.e., 6). The latter consistently had very poor power for trend detection across all strata, as has been seen at many SODN parks. By contrast, average soil stability estimates always exceeded our criteria (Table A5). Plot-level data are provided in Appendix B of the electronic version of this document.

3.2.4 Cover and frequency of biological soil crusts

Basal cover of biological soil crust growth forms and morphological groups consistently outperformed our statistical power criteria; we estimate that we will be able to detect at least a 5% change in these groups for all strata (Table A6). As is the case for vegetation data, crust frequency was not as efficient as cover, as we failed to meet our power objectives for detecting changes in the frequencies of all cyanobacteria and bryophyte-dominated crusts (Table A7). Plot-specific data are given in electronic Appendix B.

In order to help evaluate the protocol, we compared the methods of estimating biological soil crust (line-point intercept and point-quadrat) using paired t-tests in which each plot was a sample. The two sampling methods resulted in similar values for three of the four biological soil crust morphological groups. In general, the point-quadrat methodology yielded significantly higher cover of light cyanobacteria (Table 3-2).

Table 3-2. Paired t-test results for line-point intercept and point-quadrat methods for biological soil crust and substrate cover measurements at the Rincon Mountain District, Saguaro NP, 2008–2010.

Substrate	Mean difference (intercept - quadrat)		t	P
	Average	SE		
Biological soil crusts				
Light cyanobacteria	**-3.5%**	**1.5%**	**-2.39**	**0.034**
Dark cyanobacteria	-0.5%	0.4%	-1.27	0.228
Lichen	0.0%	0.4%	0.06	0.955
Bryophyte	0.1%	0.4%	0.21	0.839

degrees of freedom = 12 for all tests
Substrates for which results are statistically significant (p<0.05) are bold.
t = Student's t test statistic
P = probability of obtaining a test statistic that is at least as extreme as the observed if the null hypothesis (=no difference) is true.

4 Discussion

4.1 Are the strata effective?

After the 2009 field season, we were concerned that the lower-elevation strata (201, non-rocky sites, <3,701'; 202, rocky sites, <3,701'; and 302, rocky sites, 3,701–4500') may not be effectively partitioning variance, reducing our monitoring efficiency (Hubbard et al. 2010). To address whether the similarities were real or merely an artifact of small sample sizes, we added three plots to the 201 stratum (Cactus Forest area), and accelerated the sampling schedule for the 202 and 302 strata.

After incorporating the 2010 data, it was clear that some of the differences (201 vs. 202 or 302) were due to limited sample sizes; however, our results also indicated that plant communities in the 202 and 302 strata are actually very similar—an effect that is evident for field, subcanopy, and canopy vegetation. Aspect does not appear to explain the similarities between the two strata. However, only half of the plots in the 202 stratum have been sampled, so the similarity may be due to sample size. It is possible that these strata can be combined in the final analysis (2008–2012 data), improving our already excellent statistical power.

Overall, the strata are very effective at partitioning variance, and we are pleased with the design. Further, a flexible "evaluate and adjust as you go" approach has yielded some benefits to overall monitoring efficacy relative to traditional pilot sampling and testing approaches. In essence, the pilot work has been incorporated into the final monitoring dataset, reducing time and cost.

4.2 Does the sample size meet our criteria?

Estimated statistical power to detect change was excellent based on the proposed sample size. In fact, we at least met (and nearly always exceeded) our target criteria for change detection for perennial species. Aggregating species to lifeforms tends to decrease power by increasing the mean and variance. However, we still met our power criteria for lifeforms, with a few minor exceptions: perennial grasses in the field layer of the 302 stratum, and tree lifeforms in the canopy layer of the 502 stratum. The former would actually exceed our criteria if the 302 and 202 strata were combined, as our current results suggest (see Section 4.1). In any event, each of these lifeforms missed our change detection criteria by only 1%. From the perspective of our vegetation monitoring objectives, sample size for statistical power is excellent and does not require any adjustments.

For biological soil crust morphological groups and lichen growth forms, statistical power was even better than for vegetation, although frequency measures remain problematic—at least for cyanobacteria, an important group of crusts at Saguaro NP. As all of the morphological groups were detected via line intercepts, we will employ cover as our measure of soil crust abundance. We will continue to investigate the differences between the line-point intercept and point-quadrat methodologies for estimating biological soil crust cover.

The differences in biological soil crust cover values between the line-point intercept and point-quadrats likely stem from differences in the methodologies, proximity to the ground during measurement, and the patchiness of biological soil crust cover. The point-quadrats were placed along the line-point intercept transects such that no point-quadrat measurements actually occurred along the line-point transect. Given the patchiness of biological soil crust cover, a difference between measurement locations (the distance from the transect to the first point in the quadrat) of 5 cm could result in a different morphological group determination. Also due to the patchiness of biological soil crusts, as well as the configuration of the point-quadrats, adjacent measurements are likely to be more correlated within the quadrats (0.05-m spacing) than along the line-point intercept transects, whose measurement interval is an order of magnitude greater (0.5-m spacing). Crew members typically kneel to conduct the point-quadrat measurements, which may result in a higher observance of light cyanobacteria soil crusts. We will continue to compare the methods at Saguaro NP and other SODN parks before making a final determination between the methods for evaluating biological soil crust cover.

Power was also generally very good for soil substrate and surface soil aggregate stability measures. Slightly substandard power for a few substrate parameters in the 202 stratum may improve as additional plots are sampled and will be greatly improved by combining the 202 and 302 strata (see Section 4.1). We will focus on average stability (0–6) as our indicator of soil aggregate stability, as the alternate indicator (% of samples in very stable, or "6" category) is a very poor estimator. This is likely due to the great variance in within-plot sample size for soil stability, which tends to skew the mean and variance. We have encountered this issue at all of the SODN parks, and will drop this measure from future analyses. Overall, the sampling design is very effective for dynamic soil factors.

We detected only 336 (29%) of the 1,170 known species in the Rincon Mountain District of Saguaro NP (Powell et al. 2006). However, only 62% of the proposed sites have been sampled; the sampling frame excludes aquatic, riparian, and xeroripiarian sites that are biodiversity hotspots; and the protocol does not call for identification of annuals to species. In addition, the flattening line of the species accumulation curve suggested that our species detectability was quite reasonable. As a result, we do not recommend any increases in sample size for species detectability at this time. We will reassess this conclusion annually in future data summaries.

4.3 Implications for terrestrial vegetation and soils monitoring

This effort entailed some of the first terrestrial vegetation and soils monitoring in the SODN. Therefore, much of our focus was on evaluating the efficacy of the sampling and response designs to support improvement of the protocol. We found the plot sampling design to be efficient: most plots were sampled within 2–4 hours, including tasks that will not need to be repeated in successive visits (e.g., initial plot layout, permanent marking and mapping, and collection of in situ soil and landscape parameters).

In particular, stationing relatively large crews at Manning Camp for extended periods was an effective, safe approach for sampling less-accessible backcountry sites, whereas low-elevation sites could be efficiently measured through day trips at multiple access points. The high number of sites that failed to meet our criteria for safe access suggests that preliminary scouting of planned sites is likely a worthwhile endeavor.

After comparing these results with our monitoring objectives, we conclude that the sampling design is appropriate, and we will continue to evaluate the design through additional sampling in fall 2011. It appears likely that we may be able to reduce sampling intensity in the final year 2012 while continuing to meet or exceed our monitoring objectives.

5 Literature Cited

Bailey, R. G. 1998. Ecoregions: The ecosystem geography of the oceans and continents. New York: Springer-Verlag Inc.

Bennetts, R. E., J. E. Gross, K. Cahill, C. L. McIntyre, B. B. Bingham, J. A. Hubbard, L. Cameron, and S. L. Carter. 2007. Linking monitoring to management and planning: Assessments points as a generalized approach. The George Wright Forum 24(2):59–77.

Bingham, B. B., R. E. Bennetts, and J. A. Hubbard. 2007. Integrating science and management: the road to Rico-Chico. The George Wright Forum 24(2):21–25.

Bonham, C. D. 1989. Measurements for terrestrial vegetation. New York: Wiley-Interscience.

Clarke, K. R., and R. M. Warwick. 2001. Change in marine communities: An approach to statistical analysis and interpretation, 2nd edition. PRIMER-E, Plymouth, U.K.

Elzinga, C. L., D. W. Salzer, and J. W. Willoughby. 1998. Measuring and monitoring plant populations. Bureau of Land Management, Denver, Colorado. BLM Technical Reference 1730-1.

Herrick, J. E., J. W. Van Zee, K. M. Havstad, L. M. Burkett, and W. G. Whitford. 2005a. Monitoring manual for grassland, shrubland and savanna ecosystems. Volume 1: Quick start. USDA-ARS Jornada Experimental Range, Las Cruces, New Mexico.

——. 2005b. Monitoring manual for grassland, shrubland, and savanna ecosystems. Volume II: Design, supplementary methods, and interpretation. Tucson: University of Arizona Press.

Hubbard, J. A., C. L. McIntyre, S. E. Studd, T. W. Nauman, D. Angell, M. K. Connor, and K. Beaupré. 2009. Terrestrial vegetation and soils monitoring protocol and standard operating procedures for the Sonoran Desert Network.

Hubbard, J. A., S. Studd, and C. McIntyre. 2010. Terrestrial vegetation and soils monitoring at Fort Bowie National Historic Site: 2008 status report. Natural Resource Technical Report NPS/SODN/NRTR—2010/368. National Park Service, Fort Collins, Colorado.

McAuliffe, J. R. 1999. The Sonoran Desert: Landscape complexity and ecological diversity. Pages 68–114 *in* R. H. Robichaux, ed., Ecology of Sonoran Desert plants and plant communities. Tucson: University of Arizona Press.

National Park Service. 2005. Sonoran Desert Network monitoring plan. National Park Service, Sonoran Desert Network, Tucson, Arizona.

Powell, B. F., W. L. Halvorson, and C. A. Schmidt. 2006. Vascular plant and vertebrate inventory of Saguaro National Park, Rincon Mountain District. USGS OFR 2006-1075. USGS Southwest Biological Science Center, Sonoran Desert Research Station, University of Arizona, Tucson, Arizona.

Shreve, F. 1951. Vegetation of the Sonoran Desert. Washington, D.C.: Carnegie Institution of Washington Publication no. 591.

Stehman, S. V. 1999. Basic probabilistic sampling for thematic mapper accuracy assessment. International Journal of Remote Sensing 20:2347–2366.

Stevens, D. L., and A. R. Olsen. 2004. Spatially balanced sampling of natural resources. Journal of the American Statistical Association 99:262–278.

Theobald, D. M., D. L. Stevens, Jr., D. White, N. S. Urquart, A. R. Olsen, and J. B. Norman. 2007. Using GIS to generate spatially balanced designs for natural resource applications. Environmental Management 40:134–146.

Ugland, K. I., J. S. Gray, and K. E. Ellingsen. 2003. The species-accumulation curve and estimation of species richness. Journal of Animal Ecology 72:888–897.

Whittaker, R. H. 1975. Communities and ecosystems. Indianapolis, In.: MacMillan.

Appendix A. Supplementary Data Tables by Stratum

These data represent only 62% of the proposed sample size, and are presented to evaluate power to detect change only. Ecological conclusions should NOT be drawn from this data!

Unless otherwise noted, the following categories and notations apply throughout this appendix.

Stratum	Elevation	Description	Number of plots
201	<3,700'	Non-rocky	5 (of 5)
202	<3,700'	Very to Extremely Rocky	5 (of 11)
302	3,701–4,500'	Very to Extremely Rocky	5 (of 8)
402	4,501–6,000'	Very to Extremely Rocky	12 (of 21)
502	>6,001'	Very to Extremely Rocky	12 (of 18)
Parkwide			39 (of 63)

Layer	Stature
Field	<0.5 m
Subcanopy	0.5–2.0 m
Canopy	>2.0 m

- AVG = average
- MDC = minimum detectable change (% cover)
- n = required number of plots for power criteria
- SD = standard deviation
- Sdiff = standard deviation of the differences
- SE = standard error

- Highlighted species failed to meet our statistical power criteria.
- Bolded species are non-native.

Table A1a. Cover values (%) for species measured in the field layer of terrestrial vegetation and soils plots, low-elevation strata, Rincon Mountain District, Saguaro NP, 2008–2010.

Species	201				202				302			
	AVG	SE	MDC	n=	AVG	SE	MDC	n=	AVG	SE	MDC	n=
Forb/Herb												
Allionia incarnata	---	---	5%	0	---	---	5%	0	0.3%	0.3%	5%	1
Ambrosia confertiflora	0.1%	0.1%	5%	1	---	---	5%	0	---	---	5%	0
Antennaria marginata	---	---	5%	0	---	---	5%	0	---	---	5%	0
Artemisia ludoviciana	0.1%	0.1%	5%	1	---	---	5%	0	---	---	5%	0
Astrolepis cochisensis	---	---	5%	0	---	---	5%	0	---	---	5%	0
Bahia absinthifolia	0.1%	0.1%	5%	1	---	---	5%	0	---	---	5%	0
Boerhavia coccinea	---	---	5%	0	---	---	5%	0	0.2%	0.2%	5%	1
Bommeria hispida	---	---	5%	0	---	---	5%	0	---	---	5%	0
Brickellia betonicifolia	---	---	5%	0	---	---	5%	0	---	---	5%	0
Chamaesyce sp.	0.3%	0.3%	5%	1	0.1%	0.1%	5%	1	---	---	5%	0
Cheilanthes fendleri	---	---	5%	0	---	---	5%	0	---	---	5%	0
Cheilanthes lindheimeri	---	---	5%	0	---	---	5%	0	---	---	5%	0
Cheilanthes sp.	---	---	5%	0	---	---	5%	0	0.1%	0.1%	5%	1
Commelina dianthifolia	---	---	5%	0	---	---	5%	0	---	---	5%	0
Conyza bonariensis	---	---	5%	0	---	---	5%	0	---	---	5%	0
Conyza canadensis	---	---	5%	0	---	---	5%	0	---	---	5%	0
Dalea sp.,	---	---	5%	0	0.3%	0.2%	5%	1	1.8%	1.6%	5%	3
Daucus pusillus	---	---	5%	0	---	---	5%	0	0.1%	0.1%	5%	1
Draba helleriana	---	---	5%	0	---	---	5%	0	---	---	5%	0
Erigeron oreophilus	---	---	5%	0	---	---	5%	0	---	---	5%	0
Eriogonum abertianum	---	---	5%	0	---	---	5%	0	---	---	5%	0
Evolvulus alsinoides	---	---	5%	0	0.1%	0.1%	5%	1	---	---	5%	0
Evolvulus arizonicus	---	---	5%	0	0.2%	0.2%	5%	1	---	---	5%	0
Heuchera sanguinea	---	---	5%	0	---	---	5%	0	---	---	5%	0
Hymenothrix wrightii	---	---	5%	0	---	---	5%	0	---	---	5%	0
Ipomoea sp.	---	---	5%	0	---	---	5%	0	0.6%	0.6%	5%	1
Ipomoea ternifolia	---	---	5%	0	---	---	5%	0	0.3%	0.3%	5%	1
Koanophyllon sp.	---	---	5%	0	1.0%	1.0%	5%	1	---	---	5%	0
Machaeranthera sp.	---	---	5%	0	---	---	5%	0	0.1%	0.1%	5%	1
Mentzelia sp.	---	---	5%	0	---	---	5%	0	---	---	5%	0
Nicotiana obtusifolia	---	---	5%	0	---	---	5%	0	0.1%	0.1%	5%	1
Notholaena standleyi	---	---	5%	0	---	---	5%	0	---	---	5%	0
Oxalis sp.	---	---	5%	0	---	---	5%	0	---	---	5%	0
Packera neomexicana	---	---	5%	0	---	---	5%	0	---	---	5%	0
Pellaea wrightiana	---	---	5%	0	0.1%	0.1%	5%	1	---	---	5%	0
Pseudognaphalium canescens	---	---	5%	0	---	---	5%	0	---	---	5%	0
Pseudognaphalium canescens ssp. *canescens*	---	---	5%	0	---	---	5%	0	---	---	5%	0
Pteridium aquilinum	---	---	5%	0	---	---	5%	0	---	---	5%	0
Salvia arizonica	---	---	5%	0	---	---	5%	0	0.1%	0.1%	5%	1
Selaginella arizonica	---	---	5%	0	---	---	5%	0	0.3%	0.3%	5%	1
Selaginella rupincola	---	---	5%	0	---	---	5%	0	---	---	5%	0
Symphyotrichum sp.	---	---	5%	0	---	---	5%	0	0.3%	0.3%	5%	1
Thalictrum fendleri	---	---	5%	0	---	---	5%	0	---	---	5%	0
Tradescantia pinetorum	---	---	5%	0	---	---	5%	0	---	---	5%	0

Table A1a. Cover values (%) for species measured in the field layer of terrestrial vegetation and soils plots, low-elevation strata, Rincon Mountain District, Saguaro NP, 2008–2010, cont.

Species	201				202				302			
	AVG	SE	MDC	n=	AVG	SE	MDC	n=	AVG	SE	MDC	n=
Forb/Herb, cont.												
Verbesina encelioides	---	---	5%	0	---	---	5%	0	---	---	5%	0
Viola canadensis	---	---	5%	0	---	---	5%	0	---	---	5%	0
Woodsia plummerae	---	---	5%	0	---	---	5%	0	---	---	5%	0
Graminoid												
Aristida purpurea	0.5%	0.2%	5%	1	0.1%	0.1%	5%	1	0.1%	0.1%	5%	1
Aristida schiedeana	---	---	5%	0	---	---	5%	0	0.8%	0.7%	5%	1
Aristida sp.	---	---	5%	0	---	---	5%	0	0.3%	0.3%	5%	1
Aristida ternipes	0.3%	0.2%	5%	1	0.5%	0.3%	5%	1	2.8%	1.8%	5%	3
Aristida ternipes var. gentilis	---	---	5%	0	0.2%	0.2%	5%	1	---	---	5%	0
Blepharoneuron tricholepis	---	---	5%	0	---	---	5%	0	---	---	5%	0
Bothriochloa barbinodis	---	---	5%	0	---	---	5%	0	---	---	5%	0
Bouteloua curtipendula	---	---	5%	0	1.8%	1.8%	5%	3	5.3%	2.0%	5%	4
Bouteloua eriopoda	---	---	5%	0	---	---	5%	0	0.5%	0.5%	5%	1
Bouteloua hirsuta	---	---	5%	0	---	---	5%	0	---	---	5%	0
Bouteloua repens	---	---	5%	0	0.5%	0.3%	5%	1	0.6%	0.3%	5%	1
Bouteloua sp.	---	---	5%	0	---	---	5%	0	0.2%	0.2%	5%	1
Bromus ciliatus	---	---	5%	0	---	---	5%	0	---	---	5%	0
Bromus rubens	---	---	5%	0	---	---	5%	0	0.2%	0.2%	5%	1
Bromus sp.	---	---	5%	0	---	---	5%	0	---	---	5%	0
Carex geophila	---	---	5%	0	---	---	5%	0	---	---	5%	0
Cenchrus ciliaris	0.2%	0.2%	5%	1	1.8%	1.8%	5%	3	0.1%	0.1%	5%	1
Cyperus fendlerianus	---	---	5%	0	---	---	5%	0	---	---	5%	0
Dasyochloa pulchella	0.3%	0.2%	5%	1	---	---	5%	0	---	---	5%	0
Digitaria californica	0.8%	0.6%	5%	1	0.4%	0.2%	5%	1	1.1%	0.4%	5%	1
Elymus glaucus	---	---	5%	0	---	---	5%	0	---	---	5%	0
Elymus sp.	---	---	5%	0	---	---	5%	0	---	---	5%	0
Eragrostis cilianensis	---	---	5%	0	---	---	5%	0	0.3%	0.3%	5%	1
Eragrostis intermedia	---	---	5%	0	---	---	5%	0	0.1%	0.1%	5%	1
Eragrostis lehmanniana	---	---	5%	0	1.4%	0.9%	5%	1	0.5%	0.5%	5%	1
Eragrostis sp.	---	---	5%	0	---	---	5%	0	---	---	5%	0
Heteropogon contortus	---	---	5%	0	---	---	5%	0	0.4%	0.3%	5%	1
Leptochloa dubia	---	---	5%	0	---	---	5%	0	---	---	5%	0
Muhlenbergia alopecuroides	---	---	5%	0	---	---	5%	0	---	---	5%	0
Muhlenbergia emersleyi	---	---	5%	0	---	---	5%	0	0.1%	0.1%	5%	1
Muhlenbergia polycaulis	---	---	5%	0	---	---	5%	0	0.2%	0.2%	5%	1
Muhlenbergia porteri	3.9%	1.1%	5%	2	2.8%	1.3%	5%	2	3.7%	1.5%	5%	2
Panicum bulbosum	---	---	5%	0	---	---	5%	0	---	---	5%	0
Panicum hirticaule	---	---	5%	0	---	---	5%	0	---	---	5%	0
Panicum sp.	---	---	5%	0	---	---	5%	0	---	---	5%	0
Piptochaetium fimbriatum	---	---	5%	0	---	---	5%	0	---	---	5%	0
Piptochaetium pringlei	---	---	5%	0	---	---	5%	0	0.1%	0.1%	5%	1
Poa fendleriana	---	---	5%	0	---	---	5%	0	---	---	5%	0
Schizachyrium cirratum	---	---	5%	0	---	---	5%	0	---	---	5%	0
Setaria grisebachii	---	---	5%	0	0.1%	0.1%	5%	1	---	---	5%	0
Setaria leucopila	---	---	5%	0	---	---	5%	0	1.6%	1.6%	5%	3

Table A1a. Cover values (%) for species measured in the field layer of terrestrial vegetation and soils plots, low-elevation strata, Rincon Mountain District, Saguaro NP, 2008–2010, cont.

Species	201				202				302			
	AVG	SE	MDC	n=	AVG	SE	MDC	n=	AVG	SE	MDC	n=
Graminoid, cont.												
Setaria sp.	---	---	5%	0	---	---	5%	0	0.1%	0.1%	5%	1
Sporobolus sp.	---	---	5%	0	---	---	5%	0	0.8%	0.8%	5%	1
Sporobolus wrightii	---	---	5%	0	---	---	5%	0	---	---	5%	0
Trachypogon spicatus	---	---	5%	0	---	---	5%	0	---	---	5%	0
Subshrub												
Abutilon sp.	---	---	5%	0	0.2%	0.2%	5%	1	0.2%	0.2%	5%	1
Abutilon abutiloides	---	---	5%	0	---	---	5%	0	0.2%	0.2%	5%	1
Abutilon incanum	---	---	5%	0	0.3%	0.3%	5%	1	0.3%	0.1%	5%	1
Acacia angustissima	---	---	5%	0	---	---	5%	0	0.3%	0.3%	5%	1
Ageratina herbacea	---	---	5%	0	---	---	5%	0	---	---	5%	0
Ambrosia ambrosioides	---	---	5%	0	---	---	5%	0	0.5%	0.4%	5%	1
Ayenia filiformis	---	---	5%	0	0.5%	0.3%	5%	1	---	---	5%	0
Baccharis brachyphylla	0.3%	0.3%	5%	1	---	---	5%	0	---	---	5%	0
Bebbia juncea	0.3%	0.3%	5%	1	---	---	5%	0	---	---	5%	0
Bouvardia ternifolia	---	---	5%	0	---	---	5%	0	---	---	5%	0
Brickellia sp.	---	---	5%	0	---	---	5%	0	0.3%	0.3%	5%	1
Brickellia atractyloides	---	---	5%	0	---	---	5%	0	0.1%	0.1%	5%	1
Brickellia californica	---	---	5%	0	---	---	5%	0	---	---	5%	0
Brickellia grandiflora	---	---	5%	0	---	---	5%	0	---	---	5%	0
Brickellia venosa	---	---	5%	0	---	---	5%	0	---	---	5%	0
Comandra umbellata	---	---	5%	0	---	---	5%	0	---	---	5%	0
Dalea pulchra	---	---	5%	0	0.1%	0.1%	5%	1	---	---	5%	0
Dalea versicolor	---	---	5%	0	---	---	5%	0	---	---	5%	0
Encelia farinosa	0.7%	0.4%	5%	1	5.9%	3.2%	5%	9	0.9%	0.7%	5%	1
Ericameria laricifolia	---	---	5%	0	0.3%	0.3%	5%	1	0.8%	0.5%	5%	1
Eriogonum wrightii	---	---	5%	0	0.3%	0.2%	5%	1	0.1%	0.1%	5%	1
Galium wrightii	---	---	5%	0	---	---	5%	0	---	---	5%	0
Gymnosperma glutinosum	---	---	5%	0	---	---	5%	0	---	---	5%	0
Ipomopsis multiflora	---	---	5%	0	---	---	5%	0	---	---	5%	0
Lotus rigidus	---	---	5%	0	---	---	5%	0	---	---	5%	0
Macrosiphonia brachysiphon	---	---	5%	0	---	---	5%	0	0.3%	0.3%	5%	1
Manihot angustiloba	---	---	5%	0	---	---	5%	0	---	---	5%	0
Menodora scabra	0.3%	0.2%	5%	1	---	---	5%	0	---	---	5%	0
Nolina microcarpa	---	---	5%	0	---	---	5%	0	---	---	5%	0
Penstemon linarioides	---	---	5%	0	---	---	5%	0	---	---	5%	0
Porophyllum gracile	0.3%	0.3%	5%	1	0.3%	0.2%	5%	1	---	---	5%	0
Psilostrophe cooperi	0.1%	0.1%	5%	1	---	---	5%	0	---	---	5%	0
Rubus neomexicanus	---	---	5%	0	---	---	5%	0	---	---	5%	0
Schoenocrambe linearifolia	---	---	5%	0	---	---	5%	0	---	---	5%	0
Senna covesii	---	---	5%	0	0.1%	0.1%	5%	1	---	---	5%	0
Sphaeralcea sp.	0.1%	0.1%	5%	1	---	---	5%	0	---	---	5%	0
Trichostema arizonicum	---	---	5%	0	---	---	5%	0	---	---	5%	0
Zinnia acerosa	2.4%	0.9%	5%	1	0.1%	0.1%	5%	1	---	---	5%	0

Table A1a. Cover values (%) for species measured in the field layer of terrestrial vegetation and soils plots, low-elevation strata, Rincon Mountain District, Saguaro NP, 2008–2010, cont.

Species	201				202				302			
	AVG	SE	MDC	n=	AVG	SE	MDC	n=	AVG	SE	MDC	n=
Shrub												
Aloysia wrightii	---	---	5%	0	0.8%	0.6%	5%	1	0.2%	0.2%	5%	1
Anisacanthus thurberi	---	---	5%	0	---	---	5%	0	---	---	5%	0
Arctostaphylos pungens	---	---	5%	0	---	---	5%	0	---	---	5%	0
Baccharis sarothroides	---	---	5%	0	---	---	5%	0	---	---	5%	0
Calliandra eriophylla	---	---	5%	0	2.3%	1.2%	5%	2	1.4%	1.1%	5%	1
Calliandra humilis	---	---	5%	0	---	---	5%	0	0.5%	0.5%	5%	1
Calliandra sp.	---	---	5%	0	0.9%	0.9%	5%	1	1.0%	0.9%	5%	1
Ceanothus fendleri	---	---	5%	0	---	---	5%	0	---	---	5%	0
Ceanothus integerrimus	---	---	5%	0	---	---	5%	0	---	---	5%	0
Celtis ehrenbergiana	0.2%	0.2%	5%	1	0.1%	0.1%	5%	1	0.1%	0.1%	5%	1
Condalia sp.	0.2%	0.2%	5%	1	0.3%	0.3%	5%	1	0.3%	0.3%	5%	1
Condalia correllii	---	---	5%	0	---	---	5%	0	---	---	5%	0
Coursetia glandulosa	---	---	5%	0	1.1%	1.1%	5%	2	---	---	5%	0
Crossosoma bigelovii	---	---	5%	0	---	---	5%	0	0.3%	0.2%	5%	1
Ephedra sp.	0.1%	0.1%	5%	1	---	---	5%	0	---	---	5%	0
Ephedra trifurca	0.4%	0.4%	5%	1	---	---	5%	0	---	---	5%	0
Garrya wrightii	---	---	5%	0	---	---	5%	0	---	---	5%	0
Gossypium thurberi	---	---	5%	0	---	---	5%	0	0.2%	0.1%	5%	1
Holodiscus discolor	---	---	5%	0	---	---	5%	0	---	---	5%	0
Holodiscus dumosus	---	---	5%	0	---	---	5%	0	---	---	5%	0
Jacquemontia pringlei	---	---	5%	0	0.1%	0.1%	5%	1	---	---	5%	0
Jatropha cardiophylla	---	---	5%	0	1.7%	0.6%	5%	1	0.3%	0.2%	5%	1
Larrea tridentata	4.9%	2.8%	6%	5	---	---	5%	0	---	---	5%	0
Lycium andersonii	---	---	5%	0	0.3%	0.3%	5%	1	0.2%	0.2%	5%	1
Lycium pallidum	---	---	5%	0	0.2%	0.2%	5%	1	---	---	5%	0
Mimosa aculeaticarpa	---	---	5%	0	---	---	5%	0	---	---	5%	0
Mimosa aculeaticarpa var. biuncifera	---	---	5%	0	---	---	5%	0	0.7%	0.7%	5%	1
Robinia neomexicana	---	---	5%	0	---	---	5%	0	---	---	5%	0
Symphoricarpos oreophilus	---	---	5%	0	---	---	5%	0	---	---	5%	0
Ziziphus obtusifolia	0.1%	0.1%	5%	1	---	---	5%	0	---	---	5%	0
Succulent												
Agave palmeri	---	---	5%	0	---	---	5%	0	0.6%	0.3%	5%	1
Agave schottii	---	---	5%	0	---	---	5%	0	0.6%	0.6%	5%	1
Carnegiea gigantea	0.1%	0.1%	5%	1	---	---	5%	0	---	---	5%	0
Cylindropuntia acanthocarpa	---	---	5%	0	---	---	5%	0	0.2%	0.2%	5%	1
Cylindropuntia bigelovii	---	---	5%	0	0.3%	0.2%	5%	1	---	---	5%	0
Cylindropuntia fulgida	0.1%	0.1%	5%	1	---	---	5%	0	---	---	5%	0
Cylindropuntia leptocaulis	0.9%	0.6%	5%	1	---	---	5%	0	---	---	5%	0
Cylindropuntia versicolor	---	---	5%	0	0.1%	0.1%	5%	1	0.2%	0.1%	5%	1
Dasylirion wheeleri	---	---	5%	0	---	---	5%	0	---	---	5%	0
Echinocereus fendleri	0.1%	0.1%	5%	1	---	---	5%	0	---	---	5%	0
Ferocactus wislizeni	---	---	5%	0	0.2%	0.2%	5%	1	0.1%	0.1%	5%	1
Fouquieria splendens	---	---	5%	0	0.3%	0.3%	5%	1	0.2%	0.1%	5%	1
Mammillaria sp.	0.1%	0.1%	5%	1	---	---	5%	0	0.2%	0.1%	5%	1

Table A1a. Cover values (%) for species measured in the field layer of terrestrial vegetation and soils plots, low-elevation strata, Rincon Mountain District, Saguaro NP, 2008–2010, cont.

Species	201				202				302			
	AVG	SE	MDC	n=	AVG	SE	MDC	n=	AVG	SE	MDC	n=
Succulent, cont.												
Opuntia engelmannii	0.8%	0.5%	5%	1	2.0%	0.6%	5%	1	2.7%	1.4%	5%	2
Opuntia phaeacantha	3.8%	1.7%	5%	3	---	---	5%	0	---	---	5%	0
Opuntia sp.	0.1%	0.1%	5%	1	0.1%	0.1%	5%	1	---	---	5%	0
Yucca madrensis	---	---	5%	0	---	---	5%	0	---	---	5%	0
Tree												
Acacia constricta	2.3%	1.4%	5%	2	---	---	5%	0	---	---	5%	0
Acacia greggii	---	---	5%	0	1.3%	0.5%	5%	1	0.3%	0.2%	5%	1
Arctostaphylos pringlei	---	---	5%	0	---	---	5%	0	---	---	5%	0
Celtis laevigata	---	---	5%	0	0.5%	0.5%	5%	1	---	---	5%	0
Dodonaea viscosa	---	---	5%	0	---	---	5%	0	0.3%	0.3%	5%	1
Juniperus deppeana	---	---	5%	0	---	---	5%	0	---	---	5%	0
Parkinsonia microphylla	---	---	5%	0	0.2%	0.2%	5%	1	0.7%	0.7%	5%	1
Pinus discolor	---	---	5%	0	---	---	5%	0	---	---	5%	0
Pinus ponderosa	---	---	5%	0	---	---	5%	0	---	---	5%	0
Prosopis velutina	0.3%	0.2%	5%	1	0.3%	0.2%	5%	1	0.9%	0.6%	5%	1
Pseudotsuga menziesii	---	---	5%	0	---	---	5%	0	---	---	5%	0
Quercus arizonica	---	---	5%	0	---	---	5%	0	---	---	5%	0
Quercus emoryi	---	---	5%	0	---	---	5%	0	---	---	5%	0
Quercus gambelii	---	---	5%	0	---	---	5%	0	---	---	5%	0
Quercus hypoleucoides	---	---	5%	0	---	---	5%	0	---	---	5%	0
Quercus rugosa	---	---	5%	0	---	---	5%	0	---	---	5%	0
Vine												
Galium aparine	---	---	5%	0	---	---	5%	0	---	---	5%	0
Ipomoea barbatisepala	---	---	5%	0	---	---	5%	0	---	---	5%	0
Ipomoea coccinea	---	---	5%	0	---	---	5%	0	---	---	5%	0
Janusia gracilis	---	---	5%	0	3.3%	1.5%	5%	2	4.3%	3.1%	6%	6
Phaseolus sp.	---	---	5%	0	---	---	5%	0	---	---	5%	0
Phaseolus ritensis	---	---	5%	0	---	---	5%	0	---	---	5%	0
Lifeform												
Annual Forb	2.0%	0.6%	5%	1	5.2%	2.3%	5%	5	2.4%	1.1%	5%	2
Annual Grass	7.0%	4.0%	9%	5	1.5%	1.4%	5%	2	0.6%	0.3%	5%	1
Perennial Forb	0.5%	0.2%	5%	1	1.8%	0.9%	5%	1	4.1%	1.8%	5%	3
Perennial Grass	5.9%	1.7%	5%	3	9.7%	1.9%	5%	3	19.7%	6.5%	11%	8
Fern	---	---	5%	0	---	---	5%	0	0.1%	0.1%	5%	1
Subshrub	4.3%	0.7%	5%	1	8.1%	2.9%	5%	8	3.8%	0.7%	5%	1
Shrub	5.8%	2.5%	6%	4	7.5%	1.6%	5%	3	5.0%	0.4%	5%	1
Succulent	6.0%	1.4%	5%	2	2.8%	0.4%	5%	1	4.6%	1.6%	5%	3
Tree	2.6%	1.5%	5%	2	2.3%	0.7%	5%	1	2.2%	0.8%	5%	1
Snag	7.2%	2.3%	5%	5	9.5%	3.0%	5%	8	11.2%	3.1%	6%	6
Vine	---	---	5%	0	3.3%	1.5%	5%	2	4.3%	3.1%	6%	6
Total	34.2%	3.7%	8%	5	42.1%	4.3%	6%	11	46.6%	6.1%	10%	8

Table A1b. Cover values (%) for species measured in the field layer of terrestrial vegetation and soils plots, high-elevation and all strata, Rincon Mountain District, Saguaro NP, 2008–2010.

Species	402				502				All strata			
	AVG	SE	MDC	n=	AVG	SE	MDC	n=	AVG	SE	MDC	n=
Forb/Herb												
Allionia incarnata	---	---	5%	0	---	---	5%	0	0.0%	0.04%	5%	1
Ambrosia confertiflora	---	---	5%	0	---	---	5%	0	0.0%	0.01%	5%	1
Antennaria marginata	---	---	5%	0	0.0%	0.0%	5%	1	0.0%	0.01%	5%	1
Artemisia ludoviciana	0.5%	0.3%	5%	1	---	---	5%	0	0.2%	0.10%	5%	1
Astrolepis cochisensis	0.6%	0.6%	5%	1	---	---	5%	0	0.2%	0.17%	5%	1
Bahia absinthifolia	---	---	5%	0	---	---	5%	0	0.0%	0.01%	5%	1
Boerhavia coccinea	---	---	5%	0	---	---	5%	0	0.0%	0.02%	5%	1
Bommeria hispida	0.2%	0.1%	5%	1	0.1%	0.1%	5%	1	0.1%	0.05%	5%	1
Brickellia betonicifolia	0.1%	0.1%	5%	1	---	---	5%	0	0.0%	0.03%	5%	1
Chamaesyce sp.	---	---	5%	0	---	---	5%	0	0.0%	0.03%	5%	1
Cheilanthes fendleri	0.0%	0.0%	5%	1	---	---	5%	0	0.0%	0.01%	5%	1
Cheilanthes lindheimeri	0.1%	0.1%	5%	1	0.0%	0.0%	5%	1	0.0%	0.03%	5%	1
Cheilanthes sp.	0.3%	0.2%	5%	1	0.1%	0.1%	5%	1	0.1%	0.07%	5%	1
Commelina dianthifolia	---	---	5%	0	0.1%	0.1%	5%	1	0.0%	0.02%	5%	1
Conyza bonariensis	---	---	5%	0	0.1%	0.1%	5%	1	0.0%	0.02%	5%	1
Conyza canadensis	0.1%	0.1%	5%	1	0.0%	0.0%	5%	1	0.0%	0.03%	5%	1
Dalea sp.,	0.0%	0.0%	5%	1	---	---	5%	0	0.3%	0.22%	5%	1
Daucus pusillus	---	---	5%	0	---	---	5%	0	0.0%	0.01%	5%	1
Draba helleriana	---	---	5%	0	0.1%	0.1%	5%	1	0.0%	0.02%	5%	1
Erigeron oreophilus	---	---	5%	0	0.4%	0.3%	5%	1	0.1%	0.08%	5%	1
Eriogonum abertianum	0.0%	0.0%	5%	1	---	---	5%	0	0.0%	0.01%	5%	1
Evolvulus alsinoides	---	---	5%	0	---	---	5%	0	0.0%	0.01%	5%	1
Evolvulus arizonicus	0.1%	0.1%	5%	1	---	---	5%	0	0.1%	0.04%	5%	1
Heuchera sanguinea	---	---	5%	0	0.0%	0.0%	5%	1	0.0%	0.01%	5%	1
Hymenothrix wrightii	---	---	5%	0	0.6%	0.6%	5%	1	0.2%	0.18%	5%	1
Ipomoea sp.	0.0%	0.0%	5%	1	---	---	5%	0	0.1%	0.08%	5%	1
Ipomoea ternifolia	---	---	5%	0	---	---	5%	0	0.0%	0.03%	5%	1
Koanophyllon sp.	---	---	5%	0	---	---	5%	0	0.1%	0.13%	5%	1
Machaeranthera sp.	---	---	5%	0	---	---	5%	0	0.0%	0.01%	5%	1
Mentzelia sp.	---	---	5%	0	0.0%	0.0%	5%	1	0.0%	0.01%	5%	1
Nicotiana obtusifolia	---	---	5%	0	---	---	5%	0	0.0%	0.01%	5%	1
Notholaena standleyi	0.0%	0.0%	5%	1	---	---	5%	0	0.0%	0.01%	5%	1
Oxalis sp.	---	---	5%	0	0.5%	0.5%	5%	1	0.1%	0.15%	5%	1
Packera neomexicana	---	---	5%	0	0.0%	0.0%	5%	1	0.0%	0.01%	5%	1
Pellaea wrightiana	---	---	5%	0	---	---	5%	0	0.0%	0.01%	5%	1
Pseudognaphalium canescens	0.1%	0.1%	5%	1	---	---	5%	0	0.0%	0.02%	5%	1
Pseudognaphalium canescens ssp. *canescens*	0.3%	0.3%	5%	1	0.1%	0.1%	5%	1	0.1%	0.09%	5%	1
Pteridium aquilinum	---	---	5%	0	0.2%	0.2%	5%	1	0.1%	0.07%	5%	1
Salvia arizonica	---	---	5%	0	0.1%	0.1%	5%	1	0.0%	0.03%	5%	1
Selaginella arizonica	0.0%	0.0%	5%	1	---	---	5%	0	0.0%	0.03%	5%	1
Selaginella rupincola	0.1%	0.1%	5%	1	---	---	5%	0	0.0%	0.02%	5%	1
Symphyotrichum sp.	---	---	5%	0	---	---	5%	0	0.0%	0.03%	5%	1
Thalictrum fendleri	---	---	5%	0	0.0%	0.0%	5%	1	0.0%	0.01%	5%	1

Table A1b. Cover values (%) for species measured in the field layer of terrestrial vegetation and soils plots, high-elevation and all strata, Rincon Mountain District, Saguaro NP, 2008–2010, cont.

Species	402				502				All strata			
	AVG	SE	MDC	n=	AVG	SE	MDC	n=	AVG	SE	MDC	n=
Forb/Herb, cont.												
Tradescantia pinetorum	---	---	5%	0	0.1%	0.1%	5%	1	0.0%	0.02%	5%	1
Verbesina encelioides	0.2%	0.2%	5%	1	---	---	5%	0	0.1%	0.06%	5%	1
Viola canadensis	---	---	5%	0	0.0%	0.0%	5%	1	0.0%	0.01%	5%	1
Woodsia plummerae	---	---	5%	0	0.3%	0.3%	5%	1	0.1%	0.09%	5%	1
Graminoid												
Aristida purpurea	0.7%	0.3%	5%	1	---	---	5%	0	0.3%	0.10%	5%	1
Aristida schiedeana	0.8%	0.5%	5%	1	0.9%	0.6%	5%	1	0.6%	0.25%	5%	1
Aristida sp.	---	---	5%	0	---	---	5%	0	0.0%	0.04%	5%	1
Aristida ternipes	1.5%	0.6%	5%	1	---	---	5%	0	0.9%	0.31%	5%	1
Aristida ternipes var. *gentilis*	---	---	5%	0	---	---	5%	0	0.0%	0.02%	5%	1
Blepharoneuron tricholepis	---	---	5%	0	4.1%	3.0%	6%	14	1.3%	0.96%	5%	7
Bothriochloa barbinodis	0.1%	0.1%	5%	1	0.1%	0.1%	5%	1	0.1%	0.04%	5%	1
Bouteloua curtipendula	2.5%	0.8%	5%	2	0.2%	0.2%	5%	1	1.8%	0.49%	5%	2
Bouteloua eriopoda	---	---	5%	0	---	---	5%	0	0.1%	0.06%	5%	1
Bouteloua hirsuta	0.2%	0.1%	5%	1	0.3%	0.3%	5%	1	0.1%	0.09%	5%	1
Bouteloua repens	0.3%	0.3%	5%	1	0.2%	0.1%	5%	1	0.3%	0.11%	5%	1
Bouteloua sp.	---	---	5%	0	---	---	5%	0	0.0%	0.02%	5%	1
Bromus ciliatus	---	---	5%	0	0.2%	0.1%	5%	1	0.1%	0.04%	5%	1
Bromus rubens	**0.2%**	**0.1%**	**5%**	**1**	**---**	**---**	**5%**	**0**	**0.1%**	**0.05%**	**5%**	**1**
Bromus sp.	---	---	5%	0	0.2%	0.2%	5%	1	0.1%	0.05%	5%	1
Carex geophila	---	---	5%	0	0.1%	0.1%	5%	1	0.0%	0.04%	5%	1
Cenchrus ciliaris	**---**	**---**	**5%**	**0**	**---**	**---**	**5%**	**0**	**0.3%**	**0.24%**	**5%**	**1**
Cyperus fendlerianus	0.0%	0.0%	5%	1	---	---	5%	0	0.0%	0.01%	5%	1
Dasyochloa pulchella	---	---	5%	0	---	---	5%	0	0.0%	0.03%	5%	1
Digitaria californica	0.1%	0.1%	5%	1	---	---	5%	0	0.3%	0.11%	5%	1
Elymus glaucus	---	---	5%	0	0.0%	0.0%	5%	1	0.0%	0.01%	5%	1
Elymus sp.	---	---	5%	0	0.2%	0.2%	5%	1	0.1%	0.07%	5%	1
Eragrostis cilianensis	**---**	**---**	**5%**	**0**	**---**	**---**	**5%**	**0**	**0.0%**	**0.03%**	**5%**	**1**
Eragrostis intermedia	0.5%	0.2%	5%	1	0.3%	0.2%	5%	1	0.2%	0.09%	5%	1
Eragrostis lehmanniana	**1.6%**	**1.4%**	**5%**	**4**	**---**	**---**	**5%**	**0**	**0.7%**	**0.44%**	**5%**	**2**
Eragrostis sp.	0.0%	0.0%	5%	1	---	---	5%	0	0.0%	0.01%	5%	1
Heteropogon contortus	0.9%	0.9%	5%	2	---	---	5%	0	0.3%	0.27%	5%	1
Leptochloa dubia	0.2%	0.2%	5%	1	---	---	5%	0	0.1%	0.05%	5%	1
Muhlenbergia alopecuroides	0.8%	0.2%	5%	1	0.7%	0.5%	5%	1	0.5%	0.17%	5%	1
Muhlenbergia emersleyi	11.0%	3.3%	7%	20	6.3%	3.1%	6%	15	5.4%	1.55%	5%	16
Muhlenbergia polycaulis	---	---	5%	0	---	---	5%	0	0.0%	0.02%	5%	1
Muhlenbergia porteri	---	---	5%	0	---	---	5%	0	1.3%	0.38%	5%	1
Panicum bulbosum	0.1%	0.1%	5%	1	0.0%	0.0%	5%	1	0.0%	0.02%	5%	1
Panicum hirticaule	0.1%	0.1%	5%	1	---	---	5%	0	0.0%	0.02%	5%	1
Panicum sp.	0.4%	0.4%	5%	1	---	---	5%	0	0.1%	0.12%	5%	1
Piptochaetium fimbriatum	0.5%	0.3%	5%	1	0.1%	0.1%	5%	1	0.2%	0.10%	5%	1
Piptochaetium pringlei	---	---	5%	0	0.2%	0.2%	5%	1	0.1%	0.05%	5%	1
Poa fendleriana	---	---	5%	0	0.8%	0.8%	5%	2	0.2%	0.24%	5%	1
Schizachyrium cirratum	0.2%	0.1%	5%	1	0.8%	0.6%	5%	1	0.3%	0.18%	5%	1
Setaria grisebachii	---	---	5%	0	---	---	5%	0	0.0%	0.01%	5%	1

Table A1b. Cover values (%) for species measured in the field layer of terrestrial vegetation and soils plots, high-elevation and all strata, Rincon Mountain District, Saguaro NP, 2008–2010, cont.

Species	402				502				All strata			
	AVG	SE	MDC	n=	AVG	SE	MDC	n=	AVG	SE	MDC	n=
Graminoid, cont.												
Setaria leucopila	---	---	5%	0	---	---	5%	0	0.2%	0.20%	5%	1
Setaria sp.	0.0%	0.0%	5%	1	---	---	5%	0	0.0%	0.01%	5%	1
Sporobolus sp.	---	---	5%	0	---	---	5%	0	0.1%	0.11%	5%	1
Sporobolus wrightii	0.0%	0.0%	5%	1	---	---	5%	0	0.0%	0.01%	5%	1
Trachypogon spicatus	0.2%	0.1%	5%	1	---	---	5%	0	0.1%	0.04%	5%	1
Subshrub												
Abutilon sp.	---	---	5%	0	---	---	5%	0	0.0%	0.03%	5%	1
Abutilon abutiloides	---	---	5%	0	---	---	5%	0	0.0%	0.02%	5%	1
Abutilon incanum	---	---	5%	0	---	---	5%	0	0.1%	0.05%	5%	1
Acacia angustissima	0.8%	0.6%	5%	1	---	---	5%	0	0.3%	0.20%	5%	1
Ageratina herbacea	0.0%	0.0%	5%	1	0.1%	0.1%	5%	1	0.0%	0.02%	5%	1
Ambrosia ambrosioides	---	---	5%	0	---	---	5%	0	0.1%	0.05%	5%	1
Ayenia filiformis	---	---	5%	0	---	---	5%	0	0.1%	0.05%	5%	1
Baccharis brachyphylla	---	---	5%	0	---	---	5%	0	0.0%	0.03%	5%	1
Bebbia juncea	---	---	5%	0	---	---	5%	0	0.0%	0.04%	5%	1
Bouvardia ternifolia	---	---	5%	0	0.0%	0.0%	5%	1	0.0%	0.01%	5%	1
Brickellia sp.	---	---	5%	0	0.6%	0.3%	5%	1	0.2%	0.10%	5%	1
Brickellia atractyloides	---	---	5%	0	---	---	5%	0	0.0%	0.01%	5%	1
Brickellia californica	0.2%	0.2%	5%	1	---	---	5%	0	0.1%	0.05%	5%	1
Brickellia grandiflora	---	---	5%	0	0.3%	0.2%	5%	1	0.1%	0.08%	5%	1
Brickellia venosa	0.0%	0.0%	5%	1	---	---	5%	0	0.0%	0.01%	5%	1
Comandra umbellata	---	---	5%	0	0.1%	0.1%	5%	1	0.0%	0.03%	5%	1
Dalea pulchra	---	---	5%	0	---	---	5%	0	0.0%	0.01%	5%	1
Dalea versicolor	0.1%	0.1%	5%	1	---	---	5%	0	0.0%	0.02%	5%	1
Encelia farinosa	---	---	5%	0	---	---	5%	0	1.0%	0.50%	5%	2
Ericameria laricifolia	0.4%	0.3%	5%	1	---	---	5%	0	0.3%	0.13%	5%	1
Erlogonum wrightii	0.4%	0.3%	5%	1	---	---	5%	0	0.2%	0.09%	5%	1
Galium wrightii	0.0%	0.0%	5%	1	---	---	5%	0	0.0%	0.01%	5%	1
Gymnosperma glutinosum	0.3%	0.3%	5%	1	---	---	5%	0	0.1%	0.10%	5%	1
Ipomopsis multiflora	0.0%	0.0%	5%	1	0.0%	0.0%	5%	1	0.0%	0.01%	5%	1
Lotus rigidus	---	---	5%	0	0.0%	0.0%	5%	1	0.0%	0.01%	5%	1
Macrosiphonia brachysiphon	---	---	5%	0	---	---	5%	0	0.0%	0.03%	5%	1
Manihot angustiloba	0.1%	0.1%	5%	1	---	---	5%	0	0.0%	0.02%	5%	1
Menodora scabra	---	---	5%	0	---	---	5%	0	0.0%	0.02%	5%	1
Nolina microcarpa	4.8%	1.0%	5%	2	1.0%	0.5%	5%	1	1.8%	0.47%	5%	2
Penstemon linarioides	---	---	5%	0	0.1%	0.1%	5%	1	0.0%	0.03%	5%	1
Porophyllum gracile	---	---	5%	0	---	---	5%	0	0.1%	0.05%	5%	1
Psilostrophe cooperi	---	---	5%	0	---	---	5%	0	0.0%	0.01%	5%	1
Rubus neomexicanus	---	---	5%	0	0.1%	0.1%	5%	1	0.0%	0.02%	5%	1
Schoenocrambe linearifolia	---	---	5%	0	0.0%	0.0%	5%	1	0.0%	0.01%	5%	1
Senna covesii	---	---	5%	0	---	---	5%	0	0.0%	0.01%	5%	1
Sphaeralcea sp.	---	---	5%	0	---	---	5%	0	0.0%	0.01%	5%	1
Trichostema arizonicum	---	---	5%	0	0.0%	0.0%	5%	1	0.0%	0.01%	5%	1
Zinnia acerosa	---	---	5%	0	---	---	5%	0	0.3%	0.17%	5%	1

Table A1b. Cover values (%) for species measured in the field layer of terrestrial vegetation and soils plots, high-elevation and all strata, Rincon Mountain District, Saguaro NP, 2008–2010, cont.

Species	402				502				All strata			
	AVG	SE	MDC	n=	AVG	SE	MDC	n=	AVG	SE	MDC	n=
Shrub												
Aloysia wrightii	---	---	5%	0	---	---	5%	0	0.1%	0.08%	5%	1
Anisacanthus thurberi	0.0%	0.0%	5%	1	---	---	5%	0	0.0%	0.01%	5%	1
Arctostaphylos pungens	4.1%	1.2%	5%	4	7.0%	2.7%	5%	15	3.4%	0.99%	5%	7
Baccharis sarothroides	0.1%	0.1%	5%	1	---	---	5%	0	0.0%	0.02%	5%	1
Calliandra eriophylla	---	---	5%	0	---	---	5%	0	0.5%	0.23%	5%	1
Calliandra humilis	---	---	5%	0	---	---	5%	0	0.1%	0.06%	5%	1
Calliandra sp.	---	---	5%	0	---	---	5%	0	0.2%	0.16%	5%	1
Ceanothus fendleri	0.2%	0.2%	5%	1	0.2%	0.1%	5%	1	0.1%	0.08%	5%	1
Ceanothus integerrimus	---	---	5%	0	0.1%	0.1%	5%	1	0.0%	0.02%	5%	1
Celtis ehrenbergiana	---	---	5%	0	---	---	5%	0	0.0%	0.03%	5%	1
Condalia sp.	---	---	5%	0	---	---	5%	0	0.1%	0.05%	5%	1
Condalia correllii	0.1%	0.1%	5%	1	---	---	5%	0	0.0%	0.02%	5%	1
Coursetia glandulosa	---	---	5%	0	---	---	5%	0	0.1%	0.14%	5%	1
Crossosoma bigelovii	---	---	5%	0	---	---	5%	0	0.0%	0.02%	5%	1
Ephedra sp.	---	---	5%	0	---	---	5%	0	0.0%	0.01%	5%	1
Ephedra trifurca	---	---	5%	0	---	---	5%	0	0.1%	0.05%	5%	1
Garrya wrightii	0.8%	0.3%	5%	1	0.5%	0.3%	5%	1	0.4%	0.13%	5%	1
Gossypium thurberi	0.0%	0.0%	5%	1	---	---	5%	0	0.0%	0.02%	5%	1
Holodiscus discolor	---	---	5%	0	0.0%	0.0%	5%	1	0.0%	0.01%	5%	1
Holodiscus dumosus	---	---	5%	0	0.0%	0.0%	5%	1	0.0%	0.01%	5%	1
Jacquemontia pringlei	---	---	5%	0	---	---	5%	0	0.0%	0.01%	5%	1
Jatropha cardiophylla	---	---	5%	0	---	---	5%	0	0.3%	0.12%	5%	1
Larrea tridentata	---	---	5%	0	---	---	5%	0	0.6%	0.42%	5%	2
Lycium andersonii	---	---	5%	0	---	---	5%	0	0.1%	0.04%	5%	1
Lycium pallidum	---	---	5%	0	---	---	5%	0	0.0%	0.02%	5%	1
Mimosa aculeaticarpa	0.2%	0.1%	5%	1	0.1%	0.1%	5%	1	0.1%	0.05%	5%	1
Mimosa aculeaticarpa var. biuncifera	0.0%	0.0%	5%	1	---	---	5%	0	0.1%	0.09%	5%	1
Robinia neomexicana	---	---	5%	0	0.0%	0.0%	5%	1	0.0%	0.01%	5%	1
Symphoricarpos oreophilus	---	---	5%	0	0.1%	0.1%	5%	1	0.0%	0.04%	5%	1
Ziziphus obtusifolia	---	---	5%	0	---	---	5%	0	0.0%	0.01%	5%	1
Succulent												
Agave palmeri	0.1%	0.0%	5%	1	0.1%	0.1%	5%	1	0.1%	0.05%	5%	1
Agave schottii	2.6%	1.2%	5%	3	0.9%	0.9%	5%	2	1.1%	0.47%	5%	2
Carnegiea gigantea	---	---	5%	0	---	---	5%	0	0.0%	0.01%	5%	1
Cylindropuntia acanthocarpa	---	---	5%	0	---	---	5%	0	0.0%	0.02%	5%	1
Cylindropuntia bigelovii	---	---	5%	0	---	---	5%	0	0.0%	0.02%	5%	1
Cylindropuntia fulgida	---	---	5%	0	---	---	5%	0	0.0%	0.01%	5%	1
Cylindropuntia leptocaulis	---	---	5%	0	---	---	5%	0	0.1%	0.08%	5%	1
Cylindropuntia versicolor	---	---	5%	0	---	---	5%	0	0.0%	0.02%	5%	1
Dasylirion wheeleri	0.8%	0.3%	5%	1	0.1%	0.1%	5%	1	0.3%	0.12%	5%	1
Echinocereus fendleri	---	---	5%	0	---	---	5%	0	0.0%	0.01%	5%	1
Ferocactus wislizeni	---	---	5%	0	---	---	5%	0	0.0%	0.02%	5%	1
Fouquieria splendens	0.1%	0.0%	5%	1	---	---	5%	0	0.1%	0.04%	5%	1
Mammillaria sp.	---	---	5%	0	---	---	5%	0	0.0%	0.02%	5%	1

Table A1b. Cover values (%) for species measured in the field layer of terrestrial vegetation and soils plots, high-elevation and all strata, Rincon Mountain District, Saguaro NP, 2008–2010, cont.

Species	402				502				All strata			
	AVG	SE	MDC	n=	AVG	SE	MDC	n=	AVG	SE	MDC	n=
Succulent, cont.												
Opuntia engelmannii	0.0%	0.0%	5%	1	---	---	5%	0	0.7%	0.25%	5%	1
Opuntia phaeacantha	---	---	5%	0	---	---	5%	0	0.5%	0.28%	5%	1
Opuntia sp.	---	---	5%	0	---	---	5%	0	0.0%	0.01%	5%	1
Yucca madrensis	0.2%	0.2%	5%	1	0.2%	0.1%	5%	1	0.1%	0.06%	5%	1
Tree												
Acacia constricta	---	0.0%	5%	0	---	---	5%	0	0.3%	0.21%	5%	1
Acacia greggii	0.2%	0.2%	5%	1	---	---	5%	0	0.3%	0.11%	5%	1
Arctostaphylos pringlei	1.6%	1.6%	5%	5	0.1%	0.1%	5%	1	0.5%	0.48%	5%	2
Celtis laevigata	---	---	5%	0	---	---	5%	0	0.1%	0.06%	5%	1
Dodonaea viscosa	---	---	5%	0	---	---	5%	0	0.0%	0.04%	5%	1
Juniperus deppeana	0.0%	0.0%	5%	1	0.1%	0.1%	5%	1	0.0%	0.02%	5%	1
Parkinsonia microphylla	---	---	5%	0	---	---	5%	0	0.1%	0.09%	5%	1
Pinus discolor	0.1%	0.1%	5%	1	0.5%	0.3%	5%	1	0.2%	0.09%	5%	1
Pinus ponderosa	---	---	5%	0	0.2%	0.1%	5%	1	0.1%	0.04%	5%	1
Prosopis velutina	0.0%	0.0%	5%	1	---	---	5%	0	0.2%	0.09%	5%	1
Pseudotsuga menziesii	---	---	5%	0	0.1%	0.0%	5%	1	0.0%	0.01%	5%	1
Quercus arizonica	0.4%	0.3%	5%	1	0.6%	0.5%	5%	1	0.3%	0.17%	5%	1
Quercus emoryi	0.3%	0.1%	5%	1	0.0%	0.0%	5%	1	0.1%	0.04%	5%	1
Quercus gambelii	---	---	5%	0	0.2%	0.2%	5%	1	0.1%	0.05%	5%	1
Quercus hypoleucoides	0.3%	0.3%	5%	1	1.9%	1.2%	5%	4	0.7%	0.40%	5%	2
Quercus rugosa	---	---	5%	0	2.7%	1.8%	5%	7	0.8%	0.58%	5%	3
Vine												
Galium aparine	---	---	5%	0	0.1%	0.1%	5%	1	0.0%	0.02%	5%	1
Ipomoea barbatisepala	0.3%	0.3%	5%	1	---	---	5%	0	0.1%	0.11%	5%	1
Ipomoea coccinea	0.3%	0.3%	5%	1	---	---	5%	0	0.1%	0.10%	5%	1
Janusia gracilis	---	---	5%	0	---	---	5%	0	1.0%	0.49%	5%	2
Phaseolus sp.	0.1%	0.1%	5%	1	---	---	5%	0	0.0%	0.04%	5%	1
Phaseolus ritensis	---	---	5%	0	0.5%	0.5%	5%	1	0.1%	0.15%	5%	1
Lifeform												
Annual Forb	1.7%	0.7%	5%	1	1.7%	0.6%	5%	1	2.3%	0.45%	5%	2
Annual Grass	1.5%	0.7%	5%	1	0.6%	0.5%	5%	1	1.8%	0.65%	5%	3
Perennial Forb	2.9%	1.0%	5%	3	3.0%	1.1%	5%	3	2.6%	0.53%	5%	2
Perennial Grass	23.0%	4.2%	8%	17	15.8%	5.0%	9%	16	16.5%	2.31%	5%	36
Fern	0.2%	0.1%	5%	1	---	---	5%	0	0.1%	0.05%	5%	1
Subshrub	7.2%	1.5%	5%	5	2.5%	0.6%	5%	1	5.1%	0.71%	5%	4
Shrub	5.5%	1.3%	5%	4	8.0%	2.7%	5%	15	6.5%	0.97%	5%	7
Succulent	3.8%	1.2%	5%	3	1.4%	1.1%	5%	3	3.3%	0.60%	5%	3
Tree	2.8%	1.8%	5%	7	6.4%	2.4%	5%	12	3.8%	0.96%	5%	7
Snag	7.4%	2.0%	5%	8	6.9%	1.1%	5%	3	8.0%	0.91%	5%	6
Vine	0.8%	0.8%	5%	2	0.6%	0.5%	5%	1	1.4%	0.54%	5%	2
Total	49.3%	3.2%	6%	18	40.0%	4.9%	9%	16	43.2%	2.18%	5%	32

Table A2a. Cover values (%) for species measured in the subcanopy layer of terrestrial vegetation and soils plots, low-elevation strata, Rincon Mountain District, Saguaro NP, 2008–2010.

Species	201				202				302			
	AVG	SE	MDC	n=	AVG	SE	MDC	n=	AVG	SE	MDC	n=
Forb/Herb												
Artemisia ludoviciana	---	---	5%	0	---	---	5%	0	---	---	5%	0
Astrolepis cochisensis	---	---	5%	0	---	---	5%	0	---	---	5%	0
Boerhavia coccinea	---	---	5%	0	---	---	5%	0	0.2%	0.2%	5%	1
Conyza canadensis	---	---	5%	0	---	---	5%	0	---	---	5%	0
Dalea sp.	---	---	5%	0	0.1%	0.1%	5%	1	1.2%	1.2%	5%	2
Hymenothrix wrightii	---	---	5%	0	---	---	5%	0	---	---	5%	0
Ipomoea sp.	---	---	5%	0	---	---	5%	0	0.1%	0.1%	5%	1
Koanophyllon sp.	---	---	5%	0	0.1%	0.1%	5%	1	---	---	5%	0
Symphyotrichum sp.	---	---	5%	0	---	---	5%	0	0.1%	0.1%	5%	1
Thalictrum fendleri	---	---	5%	0	---	---	5%	0	---	---	5%	0
Verbesina encelioides	---	---	5%	0	---	---	5%	0	---	---	5%	0
Graminoid												
Aristida schiedeana	---	---	5%	0	---	---	5%	0	---	---	5%	0
Aristida ternipes	---	---	5%	0	---	---	5%	0	0.8%	0.8%	5%	1
Aristida ternipes var. gentilis	---	---	5%	0	0.1%	0.1%	5%	1	---	---	5%	0
Blepharoneuron tricholepis	---	---	5%	0	---	---	5%	0	---	---	5%	0
Bouteloua curtipendula	---	---	5%	0	---	---	5%	0	0.3%	0.2%	5%	1
Bouteloua repens	---	---	5%	0	---	---	5%	0	0.2%	0.1%	5%	1
Cenchrus ciliaris	---	---	**5%**	0	---	---	**5%**	0	0.1%	0.1%	**5%**	1
Digitaria californica	0.1%	0.1%	5%	1	---	---	5%	0	0.1%	0.1%	5%	1
Eragrostis intermedia	---	---	5%	0	---	---	5%	0	---	---	5%	0
Eragrostis lehmanniana	---	---	**5%**	0	0.1%	0.1%	**5%**	1	0.4%	0.4%	**5%**	1
Heteropogon contortus	---	---	5%	0	---	---	5%	0	0.1%	0.1%	5%	1
Leptochloa dubia	---	---	5%	0	---	---	5%	0	---	---	5%	0
Muhlenbergia emersleyi	---	---	5%	0	---	---	5%	0	0.5%	0.5%	5%	1
Muhlenbergia porteri	---	---	5%	0	0.2%	0.2%	5%	1	---	---	5%	0
Panicum sp.	---	---	5%	0	---	---	5%	0	---	---	5%	0
Piptochaetium fimbriatum	---	---	5%	0	---	---	5%	0	---	---	5%	0
Piptochaetium pringlei	---	---	5%	0	---	---	5%	0	---	---	5%	0
Schizachyrium cirratum	---	---	5%	0	---	---	5%	0	---	---	5%	0
Sporobolus sp.	---	---	5%	0	---	---	5%	0	0.1%	0.1%	5%	1
Subshrub												
Abutilon abutiloides	---	---	5%	0	---	---	5%	0	0.1%	0.1%	5%	1
Abutilon incanum	---	---	5%	0	0.1%	0.1%	5%	1	0.1%	0.1%	5%	1
Abutilon sp.	---	---	5%	0	---	---	5%	0	0.2%	0.2%	5%	1
Acacia angustissima	---	---	5%	0	---	---	5%	0	0.2%	0.2%	5%	1
Ambrosia ambrosioides	---	---	5%	0	---	---	5%	0	0.3%	0.3%	5%	1
Baccharis brachyphylla	0.1%	0.1%	5%	1	---	---	5%	0	---	---	5%	0
Brickellia californica	---	---	5%	0	---	---	5%	0	---	---	5%	0
Brickellia grandiflora	---	---	5%	0	---	---	5%	0	---	---	5%	0
Brickellia sp.	---	---	5%	0	---	---	5%	0	---	---	5%	0
Dalea pulchra	---	---	5%	0	0.1%	0.1%	5%	1	---	---	5%	0
Encelia farinosa	0.1%	0.1%	5%	1	0.8%	0.5%	5%	1	0.2%	0.2%	5%	1
Ericameria laricifolia	---	---	5%	0	---	---	5%	0	0.1%	0.1%	5%	1
Gymnosperma glutinosum	---	---	5%	0	---	---	5%	0	---	---	5%	0

Table A2a. Cover values (%) for species measured in the subcanopy layer of terrestrial vegetation and soils plots, low-elevation strata, Rincon Mountain District, Saguaro NP, 2008–2010, cont.

Species	201				202				302			
	AVG	SE	MDC	n=	AVG	SE	MDC	n=	AVG	SE	MDC	n=
Subshrub, cont.												
Koanophyllon solidaginifolium	---	---	5%	0	0.1%	0.1%	5%	1	---	---	5%	0
Nolina microcarpa	---	---	5%	0	---	---	5%	0	---	---	5%	0
Phoradendron californicum	0.2%	0.1%	5%	1	---	---	5%	0	---	---	5%	0
Rubus neomexicanus	---	---	5%	0	---	---	5%	0	---	---	5%	0
Shrub												
Aloysia wrightii	---	---	5%	0	0.3%	0.2%	5%	1	0.2%	0.2%	5%	1
Amorpha californica	---	---	5%	0	---	---	5%	0	---	---	5%	0
Anisacanthus thurberi	---	---	5%	0	---	---	5%	0	---	---	5%	0
Arctostaphylos pringlei	---	---	5%	0	---	---	5%	0	---	---	5%	0
Arctostaphylos pungens	---	---	5%	0	---	---	5%	0	---	---	5%	0
Baccharis sarothroides	---	---	5%	0	---	---	5%	0	---	---	5%	0
Calliandra sp.	---	---	5%	0	---	---	5%	0	0.1%	0.1%	5%	1
Ceanothus fendleri	---	---	5%	0	---	---	5%	0	---	---	5%	0
Ceanothus greggii	---	---	5%	0	---	---	5%	0	---	---	5%	0
Ceanothus integerrimus	---	---	5%	0	---	---	5%	0	---	---	5%	0
Celtis ehrenbergiana	0.3%	0.3%	5%	1	0.1%	0.1%	5%	1	0.5%	0.5%	5%	1
Condalia sp.	0.3%	0.3%	5%	1	0.5%	0.5%	5%	1	0.6%	0.6%	5%	1
Coursetia glandulosa	---	---	5%	0	2.2%	2.2%	5%	5	---	---	5%	0
Crossosoma bigelovii	---	---	5%	0	---	---	5%	0	0.2%	0.2%	5%	1
Ephedra trifurca	0.1%	0.1%	5%	1	---	---	5%	0	---	---	5%	0
Fendlera rupicola	---	---	5%	0	---	---	5%	0	---	---	5%	0
Frangula californica	---	---	5%	0	---	---	5%	0	---	---	5%	0
Garrya wrightii	---	---	5%	0	---	---	5%	0	---	---	5%	0
Gossypium thurberi	---	---	5%	0	---	---	5%	0	0.9%	0.5%	5%	1
Holodiscus discolor	---	---	5%	0	---	---	5%	0	---	---	5%	0
Holodiscus dumosus	---	---	5%	0	---	---	5%	0	---	---	5%	0
Jatropha cardiophylla	---	---	5%	0	0.7%	0.3%	5%	1	0.6%	0.5%	5%	1
Larrea tridentata	8.1%	4.1%	9%	5	---	---	5%	0	---	---	5%	0
Lycium andersonii	---	---	5%	0	0.7%	0.6%	5%	1	---	---	5%	0
Lycium macrodon	0.2%	0.2%	5%	1	---	---	5%	0	---	---	5%	0
Lycium pallidum	---	---	5%	0	0.3%	0.3%	5%	1	---	---	5%	0
Mimosa aculeaticarpa	---	---	5%	0	---	---	5%	0	---	---	5%	0
Mimosa aculeaticarpa var. biuncifera	---	---	5%	0	---	---	5%	0	---	---	5%	0
Robinia neomexicana	---	---	5%	0	---	---	5%	0	---	---	5%	0
Symphoricarpos oreophilus	---	---	5%	0	---	---	5%	0	---	---	5%	0
Ziziphus obtusifolia	0.1%	0.1%	5%	1	0.1%	0.1%	5%	1	---	---	5%	0
Succulent												
Agave palmeri	---	---	5%	0	---	---	5%	0	---	---	5%	0
Carnegiea gigantea	0.1%	0.1%	5%	1	---	---	5%	0	---	---	5%	0
Cylindropuntia acanthocarpa	0.1%	0.1%	5%	1	---	---	5%	0	0.3%	0.2%	5%	1
Cylindropuntia bigelovii	---	---	5%	0	0.1%	0.1%	5%	1	---	---	5%	0
Cylindropuntia fulgida	0.3%	0.2%	5%	1	---	---	5%	0	---	---	5%	0
Cylindropuntia sp.	---	---	5%	0	0.1%	0.1%	5%	1	---	---	5%	0
Cylindropuntia versicolor	0.8%	0.4%	5%	1	0.7%	0.7%	5%	1	0.6%	0.3%	5%	1

Table A2a. Cover values (%) for species measured in the subcanopy layer of terrestrial vegetation and soils plots, low-elevation strata, Rincon Mountain District, Saguaro NP, 2008–2010, cont.

Species	201				202				302			
	AVG	SE	MDC	n=	AVG	SE	MDC	n=	AVG	SE	MDC	n=
Succulent												
Dasylirion wheeleri	---	---	5%	0	---	---	5%	0	0.2%	0.2%	5%	1
Ferocactus wislizeni	---	---	5%	0	0.1%	0.1%	5%	1	---	---	5%	0
Fouquieria splendens	---	---	5%	0	1.2%	0.8%	5%	1	0.8%	0.4%	5%	1
Opuntia engelmannii	0.1%	0.1%	5%	1	0.5%	0.2%	5%	1	0.8%	0.3%	5%	1
Opuntia phaeacantha	0.3%	0.2%	5%	1	---	---	5%	0	---	---	5%	0
Yucca madrensis	---	---	5%	0	---	---	5%	0	---	---	5%	0
Tree												
Acacia constricta	5.9%	2.1%	5%	4	---	---	5%	0	---	---	5%	0
Acacia greggii	---	---	5%	0	1.3%	0.5%	5%	1	0.6%	0.4%	5%	1
Celtis laevigata	---	---	5%	0	1.5%	1.4%	5%	2	---	---	5%	0
Celtis laevigata var. reticulata	---	---	5%	0	0.1%	0.1%	5%	1	0.2%	0.2%	5%	1
Dodonaea viscosa	---	---	5%	0	---	---	5%	0	1.2%	1.2%	5%	2
Juniperus deppeana	---	---	5%	0	---	---	5%	0	---	---	5%	0
Parkinsonia microphylla	0.8%	0.5%	5%	1	1.8%	1.6%	5%	3	2.0%	1.9%	5%	4
Pinus discolor	---	---	5%	0	---	---	5%	0	---	---	5%	0
Pinus ponderosa	---	---	5%	0	---	---	5%	0	---	---	5%	0
Prosopis glandulosa	---	---	5%	0	---	---	5%	0	---	---	5%	0
Prosopis velutina	3.3%	0.8%	5%	1	3.8%	2.9%	5%	8	6.8%	3.1%	6%	6
Pseudotsuga menziesii	---	---	5%	0	---	---	5%	0	---	---	5%	0
Quercus arizonica	---	---	5%	0	---	---	5%	0	---	---	5%	0
Quercus emoryi	---	---	5%	0	---	---	5%	0	---	---	5%	0
Quercus gambelii	---	---	5%	0	---	---	5%	0	---	---	5%	0
Quercus hypoleucoides	---	---	5%	0	---	---	5%	0	---	---	5%	0
Quercus oblongifolia	---	---	5%	0	---	---	5%	0	---	---	5%	0
Quercus rugosa	---	---	5%	0	---	---	5%	0	---	---	5%	0
Quercus toumeyi	---	---	5%	0	---	---	5%	0	---	---	5%	0
Quercus turbinella	---	---	5%	0	---	---	5%	0	---	---	5%	0
Salix exigua	---	---	5%	0	0.2%	0.2%	5%	1	---	---	5%	0
Vine												
Ipomoea coccinea	---	---	5%	0	---	---	5%	0	---	---	5%	0
Janusia gracilis	---	---	5%	0	0.2%	0.1%	5%	1	0.8%	0.5%	5%	1
Phaseolus ritensis	---	---	5%	0	---	---	5%	0	---	---	5%	0
Phaseolus sp.	---	---	5%	0	---	---	5%	0	---	---	5%	0
Lifeform												
Annual Forb	0.1%	0.1%	5%	1	0.1%	0.1%	5%	1	0.3%	0.3%	5%	1
Annual Grass	---	---	5%	0	---	---	5%	0	---	---	5%	0
Perennial Forb	---	---	5%	0	0.2%	0.1%	5%	1	1.5%	1.1%	5%	2
Perennial Grass	0.1%	0.1%	5%	1	0.3%	0.2%	5%	1	2.6%	2.1%	5%	4
Subshrub	0.3%	0.2%	5%	1	1.0%	0.4%	5%	1	1.0%	0.5%	5%	1
Shrub	9.1%	4.0%	9%	5	4.8%	2.5%	5%	6	3.0%	1.8%	5%	3
Succulent	1.8%	0.7%	5%	1	2.6%	1.1%	5%	2	2.5%	0.5%	5%	1
Tree	10.0%	2.6%	6%	5	8.8%	4.5%	7%	9	10.7%	4.0%	7%	8
Snag	0.1%	0.1%	5%	1	0.3%	0.2%	5%	1	0.9%	0.4%	5%	1
Vine	---	---	5%	0	0.2%	0.1%	5%	1	0.8%	0.5%	5%	1
Total	21.3%	3.9%	9%	5	17.9%	5.1%	8%	9	22.4%	5.7%	10%	7

Table A2b. Cover values (%) for species measured in the subcanopy layer of terrestrial vegetation and soils plots, high-elevation and all strata, Rincon Mountain District, Saguaro NP, 2008–2010.

Species	402				502				Parkwide			
	AVG	SE	MDC	n=	AVG	SE	MDC	n=	AVG	SE	MDC	n=
Forb/Herb												
Artemisia ludoviciana	0.2%	0.1%	5%	1	---	---	5%	0	0.1%	0.04%	5%	1
Astrolepis cochisensis	0.0%	0.0%	5%	1	---	---	5%	0	0.0%	0.01%	5%	1
Boerhavia coccinea	---	---	5%	0	---	---	5%	0	0.0%	0.02%	5%	1
Conyza canadensis	0.1%	0.1%	5%	1	---	---	5%	0	0.0%	0.02%	5%	1
Dalea sp.	---	---	5%	0	---	---	5%	0	0.2%	0.15%	5%	1
Hymenothrix wrightii	---	---	5%	0	0.0%	0.0%	5%	1	0.0%	0.01%	5%	1
Ipomoea sp.	---	---	5%	0	---	---	5%	0	0.0%	0.01%	5%	1
Koanophyllon sp.	---	---	5%	0	---	---	5%	0	0.0%	0.01%	5%	1
Symphyotrichum sp.	---	---	5%	0	---	---	5%	0	0.0%	0.01%	5%	1
Thalictrum fendleri	---	---	5%	0	0.0%	0.0%	5%	1	0.0%	0.01%	5%	1
Verbesina encelioides	0.2%	0.2%	5%	1	---	---	5%	0	0.1%	0.05%	5%	1
Graminoid												
Aristida schiedeana	0.0%	0.0%	5%	1	0.1%	0.0%	5%	1	0.0%	0.02%	5%	1
Aristida ternipes	0.2%	0.1%	5%	1	---	---	5%	0	0.2%	0.11%	5%	1
Aristida ternipes var. *gentilis*	---	---	5%	0	---	---	5%	0	0.0%	0.01%	5%	1
Blepharoneuron tricholepis	---	---	5%	0	0.5%	0.4%	5%	1	0.1%	0.11%	5%	1
Bouteloua curtipendula	0.1%	0.1%	5%	1	0.1%	0.1%	5%	1	0.1%	0.05%	5%	1
Bouteloua repens	---	---	5%	0	---	---	5%	0	0.0%	0.01%	5%	1
Cenchrus ciliaris	---	---	5%	0	---	---	5%	0	0.0%	0.01%	5%	1
Digitaria californica	---	---	5%	0	---	---	5%	0	0.0%	0.01%	5%	1
Eragrostis intermedia	0.1%	0.1%	5%	1	---	---	5%	0	0.0%	0.03%	5%	1
Eragrostis lehmanniana	0.1%	0.1%	5%	1	---	---	5%	0	0.1%	0.06%	5%	1
Heteropogon contortus	0.2%	0.2%	5%	1	---	---	5%	0	0.1%	0.05%	5%	1
Leptochloa dubia	0.1%	0.1%	5%	1	---	---	5%	0	0.0%	0.02%	5%	1
Muhlenbergia emersleyi	1.4%	0.6%	5%	1	0.4%	0.2%	5%	1	0.6%	0.22%	5%	1
Muhlenbergia porteri	---	---	5%	0	---	---	5%	0	0.0%	0.02%	5%	1
Panicum sp.	0.1%	0.1%	5%	1	---	---	5%	0	0.0%	0.02%	5%	1
Piptochaetium fimbriatum	---	---	5%	0	0.0%	0.0%	5%	1	0.0%	0.01%	5%	1
Piptochaetium pringlei	---	---	5%	0	0.1%	0.0%	5%	1	0.0%	0.01%	5%	1
Schizachyrium cirratum	0.0%	0.0%	5%	1	0.2%	0.1%	5%	1	0.1%	0.04%	5%	1
Sporobolus sp.	---	---	5%	0	---	---	5%	0	0.0%	0.01%	5%	1
Subshrub												
Abutilon abutiloides	---	---	5%	0	---	---	5%	0	0.0%	0.01%	5%	1
Abutilon incanum	---	---	5%	0	---	---	5%	0	0.0%	0.01%	5%	1
Abutilon sp.	---	---	5%	0	---	---	5%	0	0.0%	0.02%	5%	1
Acacia angustissima	0.3%	0.2%	5%	1	---	---	5%	0	0.1%	0.06%	5%	1
Ambrosia ambrosioides	---	---	5%	0	---	---	5%	0	0.0%	0.03%	5%	1
Baccharis brachyphylla	---	---	5%	0	---	---	5%	0	0.0%	0.01%	5%	1
Brickellia californica	0.1%	0.1%	5%	1	---	---	5%	0	0.0%	0.03%	5%	1
Brickellia grandiflora	---	---	5%	0	0.0%	0.0%	5%	1	0.0%	0.01%	5%	1
Brickellia sp.	0.0%	0.0%	5%	1	---	---	5%	0	0.0%	0.01%	5%	1
Dalea pulchra	---	---	5%	0	---	---	5%	0	0.0%	0.01%	5%	1
Encelia farinosa	---	---	5%	0	---	---	5%	0	0.1%	0.07%	5%	1
Ericameria laricifolia	0.2%	0.2%	5%	1	---	---	5%	0	0.1%	0.06%	5%	1

Table A2b. Cover values (%) for species measured in the subcanopy layer of terrestrial vegetation and soils plots, high-elevation and all strata, Rincon Mountain District, Saguaro NP, 2008–2010, cont.

Species	402				502				Parkwide			
	AVG	SE	MDC	n=	AVG	SE	MDC	n=	AVG	SE	MDC	n=
Subshrub												
Gymnosperma glutinosum	0.1%	0.1%	5%	1	---	---	5%	0	0.0%	0.04%	5%	1
Koanophyllon solidaginifolium	---	---	5%	0	---	---	5%	0	0.0%	0.01%	5%	1
Nolina microcarpa	3.1%	0.8%	5%	2	0.6%	0.4%	5%	1	1.1%	0.33%	5%	1
Phoradendron californicum	0.0%	0.0%	5%	1	---	---	5%	0	0.0%	0.02%	5%	1
Rubus neomexicanus	---	---	5%	0	0.1%	0.1%	5%	1	0.0%	0.02%	5%	1
Shrub												
Aloysia wrightii	---	---	5%	0	---	---	5%	0	0.1%	0.04%	5%	1
Amorpha californica	---	---	5%	0	0.2%	0.2%	5%	1	0.1%	0.05%	5%	1
Anisacanthus thurberi	0.0%	0.0%	5%	1	---	---	5%	0	0.0%	0.01%	5%	1
Arctostaphylos pringlei	1.1%	1.1%	5%	3	0.2%	0.2%	5%	1	0.4%	0.35%	5%	1
Arctostaphylos pungens	6.3%	1.8%	5%	7	8.8%	3.1%	6%	14	4.6%	1.23%	5%	11
Baccharis sarothroides	0.1%	0.1%	5%	1	---	---	5%	0	0.0%	0.02%	5%	1
Calliandra sp.	---	---	5%	0	---	---	5%	0	0.0%	0.01%	5%	1
Ceanothus fendleri	0.3%	0.3%	5%	1	---	---	5%	0	0.1%	0.09%	5%	1
Ceanothus greggii	---	---	5%	0	0.1%	0.1%	5%	1	0.0%	0.03%	5%	1
Ceanothus integerrimus	---	---	5%	0	0.1%	0.1%	5%	1	0.0%	0.04%	5%	1
Celtis ehrenbergiana	---	---	5%	0	---	---	5%	0	0.1%	0.08%	5%	1
Condalia sp.	0.1%	0.1%	5%	1	---	---	5%	0	0.2%	0.11%	5%	1
Coursetia glandulosa	---	---	5%	0	---	---	5%	0	0.3%	0.28%	5%	1
Crossosoma bigelovii	---	---	5%	0	---	---	5%	0	0.0%	0.02%	5%	1
Ephedra trifurca	---	---	5%	0	---	---	5%	0	0.0%	0.01%	5%	1
Fendlera rupicola	0.1%	0.1%	5%	1	---	---	5%	0	0.0%	0.03%	5%	1
Frangula californica	---	---	5%	0	0.1%	0.1%	5%	1	0.0%	0.02%	5%	1
Garrya wrightii	1.7%	0.7%	5%	2	0.8%	0.6%	5%	1	0.8%	0.30%	5%	1
Gossypium thurberi	0.3%	0.2%	5%	1	---	---	5%	0	0.2%	0.10%	5%	1
Holodiscus discolor	---	---	5%	0	0.1%	0.1%	5%	1	0.0%	0.02%	5%	1
Holodiscus dumosus	---	---	5%	0	0.1%	0.1%	5%	1	0.0%	0.03%	5%	1
Jatropha cardiophylla	---	---	5%	0	---	---	5%	0	0.2%	0.08%	5%	1
Larrea tridentata	---	---	5%	0	---	---	5%	0	1.0%	0.65%	5%	3
Lycium andersonii	---	---	5%	0	---	---	5%	0	0.1%	0.08%	5%	1
Lycium macrodon	---	---	5%	0	---	---	5%	0	0.0%	0.02%	5%	1
Lycium pallidum	---	---	5%	0	---	---	5%	0	0.0%	0.04%	5%	1
Mimosa aculeaticarpa	0.5%	0.4%	5%	1	0.2%	0.2%	5%	1	0.2%	0.13%	5%	1
Mimosa aculeaticarpa var. biuncifera	0.1%	0.1%	5%	1	---	---	5%	0	0.0%	0.04%	5%	1
Robinia neomexicana	---	---	5%	0	0.1%	0.1%	5%	1	0.0%	0.02%	5%	1
Symphoricarpos oreophilus	---	---	5%	0	0.0%	0.0%	5%	1	0.0%	0.01%	5%	1
Ziziphus obtusifolia	---	---	5%	0	---	---	5%	0	0.0%	0.01%	5%	1
Succulent												
Agave palmeri	0.0%	0.0%	5%	1	---	---	5%	0	0.0%	0.01%	5%	1
Carnegiea gigantea	---	---	5%	0	---	---	5%	0	0.0%	0.01%	5%	1
Cylindropuntia acanthocarpa	---	---	5%	0	---	---	5%	0	0.0%	0.03%	5%	1
Cylindropuntia bigelovii	---	---	5%	0	---	---	5%	0	0.0%	0.01%	5%	1
Cylindropuntia fulgida	---	---	5%	0	---	---	5%	0	0.0%	0.03%	5%	1
Cylindropuntia sp.	---	---	5%	0	---	---	5%	0	0.0%	0.01%	5%	1

Table A2b. Cover values (%) for species measured in the subcanopy layer of terrestrial vegetation and soils plots, high-elevation and all strata, Rincon Mountain District, Saguaro NP, 2008–2010, cont.

Species	402				502				Parkwide			
	AVG	SE	MDC	n=	AVG	SE	MDC	n=	AVG	SE	MDC	n=
Succulent, cont.												
Cylindropuntia versicolor	---	---	5%	0	---	---	5%	0	0.3%	0.11%	5%	1
Dasylirion wheeleri	0.5%	0.2%	5%	1	---	---	5%	0	0.2%	0.07%	5%	1
Ferocactus wislizeni	---	---	5%	0	---	---	5%	0	0.0%	0.01%	5%	1
Fouquieria splendens	---	---	5%	0	---	---	5%	0	0.2%	0.12%	5%	1
Opuntia engelmannii	0.0%	0.0%	5%	1	---	---	5%	0	0.2%	0.06%	5%	1
Opuntia phaeacantha	---	---	5%	0	---	---	5%	0	0.0%	0.03%	5%	1
Yucca madrensis	0.2%	0.2%	5%	1	0.1%	0.1%	5%	1	0.1%	0.07%	5%	1
Tree												
Acacia constricta	---	---	5%	0	---	---	5%	0	0.8%	0.40%	5%	2
Acacia greggii	0.2%	0.2%	5%	1	---	---	5%	0	0.3%	0.12%	5%	1
Celtis laevigata	---	---	5%	0	---	---	5%	0	0.2%	0.18%	5%	1
Celtis laevigata var. reticulata	---	---	5%	0	---	---	5%	0	0.0%	0.02%	5%	1
Dodonaea viscosa	---	---	5%	0	---	---	5%	0	0.1%	0.15%	5%	1
Juniperus deppeana	0.6%	0.4%	5%	1	0.2%	0.1%	5%	1	0.3%	0.14%	5%	1
Parkinsonia microphylla	---	---	5%	0	---	---	5%	0	0.6%	0.33%	5%	1
Pinus discolor	0.9%	0.5%	5%	1	3.9%	1.8%	5%	7	1.5%	0.63%	5%	3
Pinus ponderosa	---	---	5%	0	0.3%	0.2%	5%	1	0.1%	0.06%	5%	1
Prosopis glandulosa	0.1%	0.1%	5%	1	---	---	5%	0	0.0%	0.03%	5%	1
Prosopis velutina	0.3%	0.2%	5%	1	---	---	5%	0	1.9%	0.64%	5%	3
Pseudotsuga menziesii	---	---	5%	0	0.4%	0.3%	5%	1	0.1%	0.11%	5%	1
Quercus arizonica	1.6%	0.7%	5%	1	1.8%	0.9%	5%	2	1.0%	0.37%	5%	1
Quercus emoryi	1.3%	0.3%	5%	1	0.5%	0.3%	5%	1	0.5%	0.16%	5%	1
Quercus gambelii	---	---	5%	0	0.3%	0.2%	5%	1	0.1%	0.08%	5%	1
Quercus hypoleucoides	0.5%	0.5%	5%	1	4.6%	2.0%	5%	9	1.6%	0.70%	5%	4
Quercus oblongifolia	0.4%	0.3%	5%	1	---	---	5%	0	0.1%	0.09%	5%	1
Quercus rugosa	---	---	5%	0	4.2%	2.6%	5%	15	1.3%	0.84%	5%	5
Quercus toumeyi	0.1%	0.1%	5%	1	---	---	5%	0	0.0%	0.04%	5%	1
Quercus turbinella	---	---	5%	0	0.1%	0.1%	5%	1	0.0%	0.02%	5%	1
Salix exigua	---	---	5%	0	---	---	5%	0	0.0%	0.02%	5%	1
Vine												
Ipomoea coccinea	0.0%	0.0%	5%	1	---	---	5%	0	0.0%	0.01%	5%	1
Janusia gracilis	---	---	5%	0	---	---	5%	0	0.1%	0.08%	5%	1
Phaseolus ritensis	---	---	5%	0	0.0%	0.0%	5%	1	0.0%	0.01%	5%	1
Phaseolus sp.	0.0%	0.0%	5%	1	---	---	5%	0	0.0%	0.01%	5%	1

Table A2b. Cover values (%) for species measured in the subcanopy layer of terrestrial vegetation and soils plots, high-elevation and all strata, Rincon Mountain District, Saguaro NP, 2008–2010, cont.

Species	402				502				Parkwide			
	AVG	SE	MDC	n=	AVG	SE	MDC	n=	AVG	SE	MDC	n=
Lifeform												
Annual Forb	0.2%	0.2%	5%	1	---	---	5%	0	0.1%	0.09%	5%	1
Annual Grass	---	---	5%	0	---	---	5%	0	---	---	5%	0
Perennial Forb	0.5%	0.4%	5%	1	0.1%	0.0%	5%	1	0.4%	0.18%	5%	1
Perennial Grass	2.3%	0.8%	5%	2	1.4%	0.5%	5%	1	1.5%	0.40%	5%	2
Subshrub	3.9%	0.9%	5%	2	0.7%	0.3%	5%	1	1.7%	0.38%	5%	1
Shrub	10.6%	2.3%	5%	12	10.8%	3.3%	6%	16	8.8%	1.41%	5%	14
Succulent	0.7%	0.3%	5%	1	0.1%	0.1%	5%	1	1.1%	0.24%	5%	1
Tree	6.0%	1.0%	5%	2	16.3%	4.7%	8%	18	10.6%	1.75%	5%	21
Snag	1.7%	0.7%	5%	2	3.4%	0.6%	5%	1	1.8%	0.34%	5%	1
Vine	0.1%	0.1%	5%	1	0.0%	0.0%	5%	1	0.2%	0.08%	5%	1
Total	24.3%	3.3%	6%	16	29.3%	5.4%	10%	16	24.4%	2.23%	5%	34

Table A3a. Cover values (%) for species measured in the canopy layer of terrestrial vegetation and soils plots, low-elevation strata, Rincon Mountain District, Saguaro NP, 2008–2010.

Species	201				202				302			
	AVG	SE	MDC	n=	AVG	SE	MDC	n=	AVG	SE	MDC	n=
Shrub												
Arctostaphylos pungens	---	---	5%	0	---	---	5%	0	---	---	5%	0
Garrya wrightii	---	---	5%	0	---	---	5%	0	---	---	5%	0
Holodiscus dumosus	---	---	5%	0	---	---	5%	0	---	---	5%	0
Larrea tridentata	0.4%	0.3%	5%	1	---	---	5%	0	---	---	5%	0
Succulent												
Carnegiea gigantea	0.2%	0.2%	5%	1	0.1%	0.1%	5%	1	0.3%	0.2%	5%	1
Cylindropuntia versicolor	---	---	5%	0	0.1%	0.1%	5%	1	0.1%	0.1%	5%	1
Fouquieria splendens	---	---	5%	0	0.3%	0.3%	5%	1	0.7%	0.2%	5%	1
Tree												
Acacia constricta	1.0%	0.5%	5%	1	---	---	5%	0	---	---	5%	0
Juniperus deppeana	---	---	5%	0	---	---	5%	0	---	---	5%	0
Parkinsonia microphylla	0.8%	0.6%	5%	1	0.1%	0.1%	5%	1	0.5%	0.5%	5%	1
Pinus arizonica	---	---	5%	0	---	---	5%	0	---	---	5%	0
Pinus discolor	0.1%	0.1%	5%	1	---	---	5%	0	---	---	5%	0
Pinus flexilis	---	---	5%	0	---	---	5%	0	---	---	5%	0
Pinus ponderosa	---	---	5%	0	---	---	5%	0	---	---	5%	0
Prosopis glandulosa	---	---	5%	0	---	---	5%	0	---	---	5%	0
Prosopis velutina	2.8%	0.8%	5%	1	1.4%	1.4%	5%	2	5.9%	4.4%	8%	7
Pseudotsuga menziesii	---	---	5%	0	---	---	5%	0	---	---	5%	0
Quercus arizonica	---	---	5%	0	---	---	5%	0	---	---	5%	0
Quercus emoryi	---	---	5%	0	---	---	5%	0	---	---	5%	0
Quercus gambelii	---	---	5%	0	---	---	5%	0	---	---	5%	0
Quercus hypoleucoides	---	---	5%	0	---	---	5%	0	---	---	5%	0
Quercus oblongifolia	---	---	5%	0	---	---	5%	0	---	---	5%	0
Quercus rugosa	---	---	5%	0	---	---	5%	0	---	---	5%	0
Quercus toumeyi	---	---	5%	0	---	---	5%	0	---	---	5%	0
Lifeform												
Annual Forb	---	---	5%	0	---	---	5%	0	---	---	5%	0
Annual Grass	---	---	5%	0	---	---	5%	0	---	---	5%	0
Perennial Forb	---	---	5%	0	---	---	5%	0	---	---	5%	0
Perennial Grass	---	---	5%	0	---	---	5%	0	---	---	5%	0
Subshrub	---	---	5%	0	---	---	5%	0	---	---	5%	0
Shrub	0.4%	0.3%	5%	1	---	---	5%	0	---	---	5%	0
Succulent	0.2%	0.2%	5%	1	0.4%	0.4%	5%	1	1.0%	0.3%	5%	1
Tree	4.7%	1.3%	5%	2	1.5%	1.6%	5%	2	6.4%	4.4%	8%	7
Snag	---	---	5%	0	---	---	5%	0	---	---	5%	0
Vine	---	---	5%	0	---	---	5%	0	---	---	5%	0
Total	5.3%	1.1%	5%	2	1.9%	1.5%	8%	1	7.4%	4.4%	8%	7

Table A3b. Cover values (%) for species measured in the canopy layer of terrestrial vegetation and soils plots, high-elevation and all strata, Rincon Mountain District, Saguaro NP, 2008–2010.

Species	402				502				Parkwide			
	AVG	SE	MDC	n=	AVG	SE	MDC	n=	AVG	SE	MDC	n=
Shrub												
Arctostaphylos pungens	0.6%	0.4%	5%	1	0.2%	0.1%	5%	1	0.2%	0.13%	5%	1
Garrya wrightii	0.1%	0.1%	5%	1	0.1%	0.1%	5%	1	0.1%	0.04%	5%	1
Holodiscus dumosus	---	---	5%	0	0.2%	0.2%	5%	1	0.1%	0.06%	5%	1
Larrea tridentata	---	---	5%	0	---	---	5%	0	0.1%	0.04%	5%	1
Succulent												
Carnegiea gigantea	---	---	5%	0	---	---	5%	0	0.1%	0.03%	5%	1
Cylindropuntia versicolor	---	---	5%	0	---	---	5%	0	0.0%	0.01%	5%	1
Fouquieria splendens	---	---	5%	0	---	---	5%	0	0.1%	0.05%	5%	1
Tree												
Acacia constricta	---	---	5%	0	---	---	5%	0	0.1%	0.08%	5%	1
Juniperus deppeana	1.5%	0.9%	5%	2	1.5%	0.7%	5%	1	0.9%	0.36%	5%	1
Parkinsonia microphylla	---	---	5%	0	---	---	5%	0	0.2%	0.10%	5%	1
Pinus arizonica	---	---	5%	0	1.7%	1.6%	5%	6	0.5%	0.49%	5%	2
Pinus discolor	1.7%	1.0%	5%	3	6.7%	3.2%	6%	15	2.6%	1.10%	5%	9
Pinus flexilis	---	---	5%	0	0.2%	0.2%	5%	1	0.1%	0.07%	5%	1
Pinus ponderosa	---	---	5%	0	6.9%	4.4%	8%	16	2.1%	1.41%	5%	14
Prosopis glandulosa	0.2%	0.2%	5%	1	---	---	5%	0	0.1%	0.06%	5%	1
Prosopis velutina	0.1%	0.1%	5%	1	---	---	5%	0	1.3%	0.64%	5%	3
Pseudotsuga menziesii	---	---	5%	0	6.1%	4.8%	9%	15	1.9%	1.51%	5%	16
Quercus arizonica	3.1%	1.1%	5%	3	2.2%	1.4%	5%	5	1.6%	0.58%	5%	3
Quercus emoryi	2.9%	1.2%	5%	3	0.6%	0.5%	5%	1	1.1%	0.44%	5%	2
Quercus gambelii	---	---	5%	0	2.1%	1.5%	5%	5	0.7%	0.48%	5%	2
Quercus hypoleucoides	0.3%	0.3%	5%	1	2.2%	0.8%	5%	2	0.7%	0.30%	5%	1
Quercus oblongifolia	0.5%	0.4%	5%	1	---	---	5%	0	0.1%	0.12%	5%	1
Quercus rugosa	---	0.0%	5%	0	2.2%	1.0%	5%	2	0.7%	0.33%	5%	1
Quercus toumeyi	0.2%	0.2%	5%	1	---	---	5%	0	0.1%	0.05%	5%	1
Lifeform												
Annual Forb	---	---	5%	0	---	---	5%	0	---	---	5%	0
Annual Grass	---	---	5%	0	---	---	5%	0	---	---	5%	0
Perennial Forb	---	---	5%	0	---	---	5%	0	---	---	5%	0
Perennial Grass	---	---	5%	0	---	---	5%	0	---	---	5%	0
Subshrub	---	---	5%	0	---	---	5%	0	---	---	5%	0
Shrub	0.7%	0.5%	5%	1	0.5%	0.2%	5%	1	0.4%	0.16%	5%	1
Succulent	---	---	5%	0	---	---	5%	0	0.2%	0.08%	5%	1
Tree	10.4%	2.0%	5%	9	32.3%	6.1%	11%	16	14.7%	2.80%	5%	53
Snag	0.5%	0.3%	5%	1	2.4%	0.7%	5%	1	0.9%	0.28%	5%	1
Vine	---	---	5%	0	---	---	5%	0	---	---	5%	0
Total	11.1%	2.4%	5%	12	32.8%	6.2%	11%	17	15.4%	2.83%	5%	54

Table A4a. Within-plot and landscape frequency (%) for all plots and species sampled on monitoring plots, low-elevation strata, Rincon Mountain District, Saguaro NP, 2008–2010.

Species	201			202			302		
	Within-plot			Within-plot			Within-plot		
	Mean (%)	SE (%)	Stratum	Mean (%)	SE (%)	Stratum	Mean (%)	SE (%)	Stratum
Forb/Herb									
Acalypha sp.	0%	0.0%	0%	0%	0.0%	0%	4%	4.0%	20%
Acourtia wrightii	0%	0.0%	0%	0%	0.0%	0%	4%	4.0%	20%
Allionia incarnata	0%	0.0%	0%	0%	0.0%	0%	24%	14.7%	60%
Amauriopsis dissecta	0%	0.0%	0%	0%	0.0%	0%	0%	0.0%	0%
Ambrosia confertiflora	16%	16.0%	20%	0%	0.0%	0%	0%	0.0%	0%
Antennaria marginata	0%	0.0%	0%	0%	0.0%	0%	0%	0.0%	0%
Arenaria lanuginosa	0%	0.0%	0%	0%	0.0%	0%	0%	0.0%	0%
Artemisia ludoviciana	16%	16.0%	20%	0%	0.0%	0%	16%	7.5%	60%
Astrolepis cochisensis	0%	0.0%	0%	0%	0.0%	0%	0%	0.0%	0%
Astrolepis sinuata	0%	0.0%	0%	0%	0.0%	0%	24%	14.7%	40%
Bahia absinthifolia	20%	12.6%	40%	0%	0.0%	0%	4%	4.0%	20%
Bidens leptocephala	0%	0.0%	0%	0%	0.0%	0%	0%	0.0%	0%
Boerhavia sp.	0%	0.0%	0%	0%	0.0%	0%	0%	0.0%	0%
Boerhavia coccinea	0%	0.0%	0%	0%	0.0%	0%	4%	4.0%	20%
Bommeria hispida	0%	0.0%	0%	0%	0.0%	0%	0%	0.0%	0%
Brickellia betonicifolia	0%	0.0%	0%	0%	0.0%	0%	0%	0.0%	0%
Centaurea melitensis	**4%**	**4.0%**	**20%**	**0%**	**0.0%**	**0%**	**0%**	**0.0%**	**0%**
Chamaesyce sp.	20%	20.0%	20%	12%	12.0%	20%	12%	8.0%	40%
Cheilanthes sp.	0%	0.0%	0%	0%	0.0%	0%	32%	16.2%	60%
Cheilanthes fendleri	0%	0.0%	0%	0%	0.0%	0%	0%	0.0%	0%
Cheilanthes lindheimeri	0%	0.0%	0%	0%	0.0%	0%	0%	0.0%	0%
Cheilanthes wootonii	0%	0.0%	0%	0%	0.0%	0%	0%	0.0%	0%
Chenopodium	0%	0.0%	0%	0%	0.0%	0%	8%	8.0%	20%
Cologania angustifolia	0%	0.0%	0%	0%	0.0%	0%	0%	0.0%	0%
Cologania pallida	0%	0.0%	0%	0%	0.0%	0%	0%	0.0%	0%
Commelina dianthifolia	0%	0.0%	0%	0%	0.0%	0%	0%	0.0%	0%
Commelina erecta	0%	0.0%	0%	0%	0.0%	0%	0%	0.0%	0%
Conyza bonariensis	0%	0.0%	0%	0%	0.0%	0%	0%	0.0%	0%
Conyza canadensis	0%	0.0%	0%	0%	0.0%	0%	0%	0.0%	0%
Dalea sp.	0%	0.0%	0%	16%	11.7%	40%	36%	22.3%	40%
Daucus pusillus	0%	0.0%	0%	0%	0.0%	0%	8%	8.0%	20%
Dieteria bigelovii	0%	0.0%	0%	0%	0.0%	0%	0%	0.0%	0%
Draba helleriana	0%	0.0%	0%	0%	0.0%	0%	0%	0.0%	0%
Drymaria leptophylla	0%	0.0%	0%	0%	0.0%	0%	0%	0.0%	0%
Dryopteris filix-mas	0%	0.0%	0%	0%	0.0%	0%	0%	0.0%	0%
Echeandia flavescens	0%	0.0%	0%	0%	0.0%	0%	0%	0.0%	0%
Erigeron oreophilus	0%	0.0%	0%	0%	0.0%	0%	0%	0.0%	0%
Eriogonum abertianum	0%	0.0%	0%	0%	0.0%	0%	0%	0.0%	0%
Euphorbia heterophylla	0%	0.0%	0%	0%	0.0%	0%	4%	4.0%	20%
Evolvulus alsinoides	0%	0.0%	0%	4%	4.0%	20%	0%	0.0%	0%
Evolvulus arizonicus	0%	0.0%	0%	8%	8.0%	20%	0%	0.0%	0%
Glandularia bipinnatifida	0%	0.0%	0%	0%	0.0%	0%	0%	0.0%	0%
Gnaphalium sp.	0%	0.0%	0%	0%	0.0%	0%	4%	4.0%	20%

Table A4a. Within-plot and landscape frequency (%) for all plots and species sampled on monitoring plots, low-elevation strata, Rincon Mountain District, Saguaro NP, 2008–2010, cont.

	201			202			302		
	Within-plot			Within-plot			Within-plot		
Species	Mean (%)	SE (%)	Stratum	Mean (%)	SE (%)	Stratum	Mean (%)	SE (%)	Stratum
Forb/Herb, cont.									
Hedeoma dentata	0%	0.0%	0%	0%	0.0%	0%	0%	0.0%	0%
Hedeoma hyssopifolia	0%	0.0%	0%	0%	0.0%	0%	0%	0.0%	0%
Hedeoma nana	0%	0.0%	0%	0%	0.0%	0%	0%	0.0%	0%
Heterotheca sp.	0%	0.0%	0%	0%	0.0%	0%	0%	0.0%	0%
Heuchera sp.	0%	0.0%	0%	0%	0.0%	0%	0%	0.0%	0%
Heuchera sanguinea	0%	0.0%	0%	0%	0.0%	0%	0%	0.0%	0%
Hymenothrix wrightii	0%	0.0%	0%	0%	0.0%	0%	0%	0.0%	0%
Ipomoea sp.	0%	0.0%	0%	0%	0.0%	0%	24%	19.4%	40%
Ipomoea ternifolia	0%	0.0%	0%	0%	0.0%	0%	20%	20.0%	20%
Justicia longii	0%	0.0%	0%	0%	0.0%	0%	4%	4.0%	20%
Koanophyllon	0%	0.0%	0%	16%	16.0%	20%	0%	0.0%	0%
Linum neomexicanum	0%	0.0%	0%	0%	0.0%	0%	0%	0.0%	0%
Lithospermum multiflorum	0%	0.0%	0%	0%	0.0%	0%	0%	0.0%	0%
Lotus sp.	0%	0.0%	0%	0%	0.0%	0%	0%	0.0%	0%
Machaeranthera	0%	0.0%	0%	0%	0.0%	0%	4%	4.0%	20%
Machaeranthera tagetina	0%	0.0%	0%	0%	0.0%	0%	0%	0.0%	0%
Macroptilium gibbosifolium	0%	0.0%	0%	0%	0.0%	0%	0%	0.0%	0%
Malaxis soulei	0%	0.0%	0%	0%	0.0%	0%	0%	0.0%	0%
Mentzelia sp.	0%	0.0%	0%	0%	0.0%	0%	0%	0.0%	0%
Monarda citriodora ssp. *austromontana*	0%	0.0%	0%	0%	0.0%	0%	0%	0.0%	0%
ANNUAL FORB	48%	13.6%	80%	64%	17.2%	80%	48%	12.0%	100%
Nicotiana obtusifolia	4%	4.0%	20%	0%	0.0%	0%	0%	0.0%	0%
Notholaena standleyi	0%	0.0%	0%	16%	11.7%	40%	4%	4.0%	20%
Oxalis sp.	0%	0.0%	0%	0%	0.0%	0%	0%	0.0%	0%
Packera neomexicana	0%	0.0%	0%	0%	0.0%	0%	0%	0.0%	0%
Pellaea sp.	0%	0.0%	0%	0%	0.0%	0%	24%	19.4%	40%
Pellaea truncata	0%	0.0%	0%	0%	0.0%	0%	24%	11.7%	60%
Pellaea wrightiana	0%	0.0%	0%	8%	8.0%	20%	0%	0.0%	0%
Penstemon barbatus	0%	0.0%	0%	0%	0.0%	0%	0%	0.0%	0%
Pseudognaphalium canescens	0%	0.0%	0%	0%	0.0%	0%	4%	4.0%	20%
Pseudognaphalium canescens ssp. *canescens*	0%	0.0%	0%	0%	0.0%	0%	0%	0.0%	0%
Pseudognaphalium leucocephalum	0%	0.0%	0%	0%	0.0%	0%	0%	0.0%	0%
Pteridium aquilinum	0%	0.0%	0%	0%	0.0%	0%	0%	0.0%	0%
Salvia arizonica	0%	0.0%	0%	0%	0.0%	0%	4%	4.0%	20%
Scrophularia parviflora	0%	0.0%	0%	0%	0.0%	0%	0%	0.0%	0%
Sedum cockerellii	0%	0.0%	0%	0%	0.0%	0%	0%	0.0%	0%
Selaginella arizonica	0%	0.0%	0%	0%	0.0%	0%	16%	16.0%	20%
Selaginella rupincola	0%	0.0%	0%	0%	0.0%	0%	0%	0.0%	0%
Solidago velutina	0%	0.0%	0%	0%	0.0%	0%	0%	0.0%	0%
Stachys coccinea	0%	0.0%	0%	0%	0.0%	0%	0%	0.0%	0%
Symphyotrichum	0%	0.0%	0%	0%	0.0%	0%	16%	16.0%	20%

Table A4a. Within-plot and landscape frequency (%) for all plots and species sampled on monitoring plots, low-elevation strata, Rincon Mountain District, Saguaro NP, 2008–2010, cont.

Species	201 Within-plot Mean (%)	SE (%)	Stratum	202 Within-plot Mean (%)	SE (%)	Stratum	302 Within-plot Mean (%)	SE (%)	Stratum
Forb/Herb, cont.									
Thalictrum fendleri	0%	0.0%	0%	0%	0.0%	0%	0%	0.0%	0%
Tradescantia pinetorum	0%	0.0%	0%	0%	0.0%	0%	0%	0.0%	0%
Verbesina encelioides	0%	0.0%	0%	0%	0.0%	0%	0%	0.0%	0%
Viola canadensis	0%	0.0%	0%	0%	0.0%	0%	0%	0.0%	0%
Woodsia plummerae	0%	0.0%	0%	0%	0.0%	0%	0%	0.0%	0%
Xanthisma gracile	0%	0.0%	0%	0%	0.0%	0%	0%	0.0%	0%
Graminoid									
Aristida sp.	0%	0.0%	0%	0%	0.0%	0%	8%	8.0%	20%
Aristida purpurea	56%	19.4%	80%	4%	4.0%	20%	8%	4.9%	40%
Aristida schiedeana	0%	0.0%	0%	0%	0.0%	0%	40%	21.0%	60%
Aristida ternipes	28%	4.9%	100%	24%	11.7%	60%	64%	19.4%	80%
Aristida ternipes var. gentilis	0%	0.0%	0%	12%	12.0%	20%	0%	0.0%	0%
Blepharoneuron tricholepis	0%	0.0%	0%	0%	0.0%	0%	0%	0.0%	0%
Bothriochloa barbinodis	0%	0.0%	0%	0%	0.0%	0%	4%	4.0%	20%
Bouteloua sp.	0%	0.0%	0%	0%	0.0%	0%	4%	4.0%	20%
Bouteloua aristidoides	0%	0.0%	0%	0%	0.0%	0%	0%	0.0%	0%
Bouteloua curtipendula	0%	0.0%	0%	16%	16.0%	20%	92%	4.9%	100%
Bouteloua eriopoda	0%	0.0%	0%	0%	0.0%	0%	8%	8.0%	20%
Bouteloua gracilis	0%	0.0%	0%	0%	0.0%	0%	0%	0.0%	0%
Bouteloua hirsuta	0%	0.0%	0%	0%	0.0%	0%	4%	4.0%	20%
Bouteloua repens	0%	0.0%	0%	56%	20.4%	80%	64%	7.5%	100%
Bromus sp.	0%	0.0%	0%	0%	0.0%	0%	4%	4.0%	20%
Bromus ciliatus	0%	0.0%	0%	0%	0.0%	0%	0%	0.0%	0%
Bromus rubens	0%	0.0%	0%	0%	0.0%	0%	24%	9.8%	60%
Carex geophila	0%	0.0%	0%	0%	0.0%	0%	0%	0.0%	0%
Cenchrus ciliaris	8%	8.0%	20%	20%	20.0%	20%	8%	8.0%	20%
Chloris virgata	0%	0.0%	0%	0%	0.0%	0%	0%	0.0%	0%
Cyperus fendlerianus	0%	0.0%	0%	0%	0.0%	0%	0%	0.0%	0%
Dasyochloa pulchella	32%	10.2%	80%	0%	0.0%	0%	0%	0.0%	0%
Digitaria californica	36%	19.4%	60%	20%	11.0%	60%	52%	10.2%	100%
Echinochloa sp.	0%	0.0%	0%	8%	8.0%	20%	12%	4.9%	60%
Elymus sp.	0%	0.0%	0%	0%	0.0%	0%	0%	0.0%	0%
Eragrostis sp.	0%	0.0%	0%	0%	0.0%	0%	0%	0.0%	0%
Eragrostis cilianensis	0%	0.0%	0%	0%	0.0%	0%	8%	8.0%	20%
Eragrostis intermedia	0%	0.0%	0%	0%	0.0%	0%	12%	12.0%	20%
Eragrostis lehmanniana	0%	0.0%	0%	52%	21.5%	60%	32%	19.6%	40%
Eriochloa lemmonii	0%	0.0%	0%	0%	0.0%	0%	0%	0.0%	0%
Heteropogon contortus	0%	0.0%	0%	4%	4.0%	20%	44%	17.2%	80%
Koeleria macrantha	0%	0.0%	0%	0%	0.0%	0%	0%	0.0%	0%
Leptochloa dubia	0%	0.0%	0%	0%	0.0%	0%	0%	0.0%	0%
Muhlenbergia alopecuroides	0%	0.0%	0%	0%	0.0%	0%	0%	0.0%	0%
Muhlenbergia emersleyi	0%	0.0%	0%	0%	0.0%	0%	12%	12.0%	20%
Muhlenbergia polycaulis	0%	0.0%	0%	0%	0.0%	0%	8%	8.0%	20%

Table A4a. Within-plot and landscape frequency (%) for all plots and species sampled on monitoring plots, low-elevation strata, Rincon Mountain District, Saguaro NP, 2008–2010, cont.

Species	201 Within-plot Mean (%)	SE (%)	Stratum	202 Within-plot Mean (%)	SE (%)	Stratum	302 Within-plot Mean (%)	SE (%)	Stratum
Graminoid, cont.									
Muhlenbergia porteri	96%	4.0%	100%	64%	13.3%	100%	60%	16.7%	100%
ANNUAL GRASS	36%	18.3%	60%	24%	19.4%	40%	12%	8.0%	40%
Panicum sp.	0%	0.0%	0%	0%	0.0%	0%	0%	0.0%	0%
Panicum bulbosum	0%	0.0%	0%	0%	0.0%	0%	0%	0.0%	0%
Panicum hirticaule	0%	0.0%	0%	0%	0.0%	0%	0%	0.0%	0%
Piptochaetium fimbriatum	0%	0.0%	0%	0%	0.0%	0%	0%	0.0%	0%
Piptochaetium pringlei	0%	0.0%	0%	0%	0.0%	0%	4%	4.0%	20%
Poa fendleriana	0%	0.0%	0%	0%	0.0%	0%	0%	0.0%	0%
Schizachyrium cirratum	0%	0.0%	0%	0%	0.0%	0%	4%	4.0%	20%
Setaria sp.	0%	0.0%	0%	0%	0.0%	0%	4%	4.0%	20%
Setaria grisebachii	0%	0.0%	0%	8%	8.0%	20%	0%	0.0%	0%
Setaria leucopila	0%	0.0%	0%	0%	0.0%	0%	20%	20.0%	20%
Sporobolus	0%	0.0%	0%	0%	0.0%	0%	12%	12.0%	20%
Sporobolus wrightii	0%	0.0%	0%	0%	0.0%	0%	0%	0.0%	0%
Trachypogon spicatus	0%	0.0%	0%	0%	0.0%	0%	0%	0.0%	0%
Subshrub									
Abutilon sp.	0%	0.0%	0%	4%	4.0%	20%	20%	20.0%	20%
Abutilon abutiloides	0%	0.0%	0%	0%	0.0%	0%	12%	12.0%	20%
Abutilon incanum	0%	0.0%	0%	40%	19.0%	60%	32%	18.5%	60%
Acacia angustissima	0%	0.0%	0%	0%	0.0%	0%	12%	8.0%	40%
Adenophyllum porophylloides	4%	4.0%	20%	0%	0.0%	0%	0%	0.0%	0%
Ageratina herbacea	0%	0.0%	0%	0%	0.0%	0%	0%	0.0%	0%
Ambrosia ambrosioides	0%	0.0%	0%	12%	12.0%	20%	32%	18.5%	60%
Ambrosia deltoidea	4%	4.0%	20%	0%	0.0%	0%	0%	0.0%	0%
Ayenia filiformis	0%	0.0%	0%	24%	19.4%	40%	4%	4.0%	20%
Baccharis brachyphylla	16%	9.8%	40%	0%	0.0%	0%	0%	0.0%	0%
Bebbia juncea	16%	11.7%	40%	0%	0.0%	0%	8%	8.0%	20%
Bouvardia ternifolia	0%	0.0%	0%	0%	0.0%	0%	0%	0.0%	0%
Brickellia	0%	0.0%	0%	8%	8.0%	20%	12%	8.0%	40%
Brickellia californica	0%	0.0%	0%	0%	0.0%	0%	0%	0.0%	0%
Brickellia grandiflora	0%	0.0%	0%	0%	0.0%	0%	0%	0.0%	0%
Brickellia simplex	0%	0.0%	0%	0%	0.0%	0%	0%	0.0%	0%
Brickellia venosa	0%	0.0%	0%	0%	0.0%	0%	0%	0.0%	0%
Comandra umbellata	0%	0.0%	0%	0%	0.0%	0%	0%	0.0%	0%
Dalea albiflora	0%	0.0%	0%	0%	0.0%	0%	0%	0.0%	0%
Dalea candida	0%	0.0%	0%	0%	0.0%	0%	0%	0.0%	0%
Dalea lumholtzii	0%	0.0%	0%	0%	0.0%	0%	0%	0.0%	0%
Dalea pulchra	0%	0.0%	0%	16%	16.0%	20%	0%	0.0%	0%
Dalea versicolor	0%	0.0%	0%	0%	0.0%	0%	0%	0.0%	0%
Encelia farinosa	40%	14.1%	80%	88%	12.0%	100%	44%	16.0%	80%
Ericameria laricifolia	0%	0.0%	0%	24%	14.7%	60%	68%	16.2%	100%
Erigeron speciosus	0%	0.0%	0%	0%	0.0%	0%	0%	0.0%	0%
Eriogonum wrightii	0%	0.0%	0%	28%	13.6%	60%	12%	4.9%	60%

Species	201 Within-plot Mean (%)	SE (%)	Stratum	202 Within-plot Mean (%)	SE (%)	Stratum	302 Within-plot Mean (%)	SE (%)	Stratum
Subshrub, cont.									
Galium stellatum	0%	0.0%	0%	0%	0.0%	0%	0%	0.0%	0%
Galium wrightii	0%	0.0%	0%	0%	0.0%	0%	0%	0.0%	0%
Geranium caespitosum	0%	0.0%	0%	0%	0.0%	0%	0%	0.0%	0%
Gutierrezia sarothrae	0%	0.0%	0%	0%	0.0%	0%	0%	0.0%	0%
Gymnosperma glutinosum	0%	0.0%	0%	0%	0.0%	0%	0%	0.0%	0%
Hibiscus biseptus	0%	0.0%	0%	0%	0.0%	0%	20%	20.0%	20%
Hibiscus coulteri	0%	0.0%	0%	0%	0.0%	0%	16%	16.0%	20%
Ipomopsis multiflora	0%	0.0%	0%	0%	0.0%	0%	0%	0.0%	0%
Isocoma tenuisecta	16%	16.0%	20%	8%	8.0%	20%	0%	0.0%	0%
Lotus rigidus	0%	0.0%	0%	0%	0.0%	0%	0%	0.0%	0%
Macrosiphonia brachysiphon	0%	0.0%	0%	0%	0.0%	0%	12%	12.0%	20%
Manihot angustiloba	0%	0.0%	0%	0%	0.0%	0%	0%	0.0%	0%
Menodora scabra	24%	19.4%	40%	0%	0.0%	0%	0%	0.0%	0%
Nolina microcarpa	0%	0.0%	0%	0%	0.0%	0%	4%	4.0%	20%
Penstemon linarioides	0%	0.0%	0%	0%	0.0%	0%	0%	0.0%	0%
Perityle lemmonii	0%	0.0%	0%	0%	0.0%	0%	0%	0.0%	0%
Phoradendron californicum	40%	12.6%	80%	0%	0.0%	0%	0%	0.0%	0%
Phoradendron villosum	0%	0.0%	0%	0%	0.0%	0%	0%	0.0%	0%
Porophyllum gracile	20%	20.0%	20%	20%	15.5%	40%	4%	4.0%	20%
Psilostrophe cooperi	28%	15.0%	60%	0%	0.0%	0%	0%	0.0%	0%
Rubus neomexicanus	0%	0.0%	0%	0%	0.0%	0%	0%	0.0%	0%
Schoenocrambe linearifolia	0%	0.0%	0%	0%	0.0%	0%	0%	0.0%	0%
Senna covesii	0%	0.0%	0%	12%	8.0%	40%	0%	0.0%	0%
Sphaeralcea	16%	11.7%	40%	4%	4.0%	20%	8%	8.0%	20%
Tagetes lemmonii	0%	0.0%	0%	0%	0.0%	0%	0%	0.0%	0%
Talinum paniculatum	0%	0.0%	0%	4%	4.0%	20%	0%	0.0%	0%
Tetramerium nervosum	0%	0.0%	0%	0%	0.0%	0%	4%	4.0%	20%
Trichostema arizonicum	0%	0.0%	0%	0%	0.0%	0%	0%	0.0%	0%
Trixis californica	0%	0.0%	0%	32%	8.0%	100%	20%	11.0%	60%
Xanthisma spinulosum	12%	12.0%	20%	0%	0.0%	0%	0%	0.0%	0%
Zinnia acerosa	52%	17.4%	80%	16%	11.7%	40%	4%	4.0%	20%
Zinnia grandiflora	36%	19.4%	60%	0%	0.0%	0%	0%	0.0%	0%
Shrub									
Aloysia wrightii	0%	0.0%	0%	24%	14.7%	60%	12%	8.0%	40%
Amorpha californica	0%	0.0%	0%	0%	0.0%	0%	0%	0.0%	0%
Anisacanthus thurberi	0%	0.0%	0%	0%	0.0%	0%	4%	4.0%	20%
Arctostaphylos pungens	0%	0.0%	0%	0%	0.0%	0%	0%	0.0%	0%
Baccharis	0%	0.0%	0%	0%	0.0%	0%	0%	0.0%	0%
Baccharis sarothroides	0%	0.0%	0%	0%	0.0%	0%	0%	0.0%	0%
Berberis wilcoxii	0%	0.0%	0%	0%	0.0%	0%	0%	0.0%	0%
Calliandra sp.	0%	0.0%	0%	20%	20.0%	20%	28%	19.6%	40%
Calliandra eriophylla	8%	4.9%	40%	56%	23.2%	60%	36%	22.3%	40%
Calliandra humilis	0%	0.0%	0%	0%	0.0%	0%	20%	20.0%	20%

| | 201 | | | 202 | | | 302 | | |
| | Within-plot | | | Within-plot | | | Within-plot | | |
Species	Mean (%)	SE (%)	Stratum	Mean (%)	SE (%)	Stratum	Mean (%)	SE (%)	Stratum
Shrub, cont.									
Ceanothus fendleri	0%	0.0%	0%	0%	0.0%	0%	0%	0.0%	0%
Ceanothus greggii	0%	0.0%	0%	0%	0.0%	0%	0%	0.0%	0%
Ceanothus integerrimus	0%	0.0%	0%	0%	0.0%	0%	0%	0.0%	0%
Celtis ehrenbergiana	8%	4.9%	40%	4%	4.0%	20%	12%	12.0%	20%
Condalia	16%	16.0%	20%	20%	20.0%	20%	12%	8.0%	40%
Condalia correllii	0%	0.0%	0%	0%	0.0%	0%	0%	0.0%	0%
Condalia warnockii	12%	8.0%	40%	0%	0.0%	0%	0%	0.0%	0%
Coursetia glandulosa	0%	0.0%	0%	12%	12.0%	20%	0%	0.0%	0%
Crossosoma bigelovii	0%	0.0%	0%	0%	0.0%	0%	32%	16.2%	60%
Ephedra sp.	8%	4.9%	40%	0%	0.0%	0%	0%	0.0%	0%
Ephedra trifurca	28%	19.6%	40%	0%	0.0%	0%	0%	0.0%	0%
Eriodictyon angustifolium	0%	0.0%	0%	0%	0.0%	0%	0%	0.0%	0%
Fendlera rupicola	0%	0.0%	0%	0%	0.0%	0%	0%	0.0%	0%
Fouquieria splendens	0%	0.0%	0%	64%	22.3%	80%	56%	17.2%	80%
Frangula californica	0%	0.0%	0%	0%	0.0%	0%	0%	0.0%	0%
Garrya wrightii	0%	0.0%	0%	0%	0.0%	0%	0%	0.0%	0%
Gossypium thurberi	0%	0.0%	0%	0%	0.0%	0%	40%	19.0%	60%
Holodiscus discolor	0%	0.0%	0%	0%	0.0%	0%	0%	0.0%	0%
Holodiscus dumosus	0%	0.0%	0%	0%	0.0%	0%	0%	0.0%	0%
Jacquemontia pringlei	0%	0.0%	0%	8%	8.0%	20%	0%	0.0%	0%
Jatropha cardiophylla	0%	0.0%	0%	68%	16.2%	100%	48%	16.2%	80%
Larrea tridentata	68%	20.6%	80%	4%	4.0%	20%	0%	0.0%	0%
Lycium	4%	4.0%	20%	12%	8.0%	40%	4%	4.0%	20%
Lycium andersonii	0%	0.0%	0%	28%	17.4%	40%	20%	20.0%	20%
Lycium berlandieri	8%	8.0%	20%	0%	0.0%	0%	0%	0.0%	0%
Lycium pallidum	0%	0.0%	0%	16%	16.0%	20%	0%	0.0%	0%
Matelea parvifolia	4%	4.0%	20%	0%	0.0%	0%	0%	0.0%	0%
Mimosa aculeaticarpa	0%	0.0%	0%	0%	0.0%	0%	0%	0.0%	0%
Mimosa aculeaticarpa var. biuncifera	0%	0.0%	0%	0%	0.0%	0%	8%	8.0%	20%
SNAG	80%	8.9%	100%	96%	4.0%	100%	88%	8.0%	100%
Plumbago zeylanica	0%	0.0%	0%	0%	0.0%	0%	8%	8.0%	20%
Rhus aromatica	0%	0.0%	0%	0%	0.0%	0%	0%	0.0%	0%
Robinia neomexicana	0%	0.0%	0%	0%	0.0%	0%	0%	0.0%	0%
Symphoricarpos	0%	0.0%	0%	0%	0.0%	0%	0%	0.0%	0%
Symphoricarpos oreophilus	0%	0.0%	0%	0%	0.0%	0%	0%	0.0%	0%
Ziziphus obtusifolia	16%	11.7%	40%	8%	8.0%	20%	12%	12.0%	20%
Succulent									
Agave palmeri	0%	0.0%	0%	4%	4.0%	20%	56%	19.4%	80%
Agave parryi	0%	0.0%	0%	0%	0.0%	0%	0%	0.0%	0%
Agave schottii	0%	0.0%	0%	0%	0.0%	0%	20%	20.0%	20%
Carnegiea gigantea	28%	10.2%	80%	44%	19.4%	80%	40%	19.0%	60%
Cylindropuntia sp.	0%	0.0%	0%	32%	20.6%	40%	0%	0.0%	0%

Table A4a. Within-plot and landscape frequency (%) for all plots and species sampled on monitoring plots, low-elevation strata, Rincon Mountain District, Saguaro NP, 2008–2010, cont.

Species	201 Within-plot Mean (%)	SE (%)	Stratum	202 Within-plot Mean (%)	SE (%)	Stratum	302 Within-plot Mean (%)	SE (%)	Stratum
Succulent, cont.									
Cylindropuntia acanthocarpa	4%	4.0%	20%	0%	0.0%	0%	36%	22.3%	40%
Cylindropuntia arbuscula	8%	4.9%	40%	0%	0.0%	0%	0%	0.0%	0%
Cylindropuntia bigelovii	0%	0.0%	0%	28%	19.6%	40%	0%	0.0%	0%
Cylindropuntia fulgida	32%	20.6%	40%	0%	0.0%	0%	0%	0.0%	0%
Cylindropuntia fulgida var. *mamillata*	4%	4.0%	20%	0%	0.0%	0%	0%	0.0%	0%
Cylindropuntia leptocaulis	48%	16.2%	80%	4%	4.0%	20%	0%	0.0%	0%
Cylindropuntia spinosior	0%	0.0%	0%	4%	4.0%	20%	0%	0.0%	0%
Cylindropuntia versicolor	36%	19.4%	60%	40%	21.0%	60%	52%	21.5%	60%
Dasylirion wheeleri	0%	0.0%	0%	4%	4.0%	20%	32%	15.0%	60%
Echinocereus sp.	8%	8.0%	20%	0%	0.0%	0%	0%	0.0%	0%
Echinocereus fendleri	20%	12.6%	40%	0%	0.0%	0%	0%	0.0%	0%
Echinocereus pectinatus	0%	0.0%	0%	0%	0.0%	0%	0%	0.0%	0%
Echinocereus rigidissimus	0%	0.0%	0%	0%	0.0%	0%	0%	0.0%	0%
Echinocereus triglochidiatus	0%	0.0%	0%	0%	0.0%	0%	0%	0.0%	0%
Escobaria vivipara	0%	0.0%	0%	0%	0.0%	0%	0%	0.0%	0%
Ferocactus wislizeni	52%	17.4%	80%	76%	7.5%	100%	56%	9.8%	100%
Mammillaria	16%	16.0%	20%	56%	17.2%	80%	32%	15.0%	60%
Mammillaria grahamii	40%	16.7%	60%	0%	0.0%	0%	20%	15.5%	40%
Opuntia	4%	4.0%	20%	4%	4.0%	20%	0%	0.0%	0%
Opuntia chlorotica	0%	0.0%	0%	0%	0.0%	0%	0%	0.0%	0%
Opuntia engelmannii	36%	18.3%	60%	84%	11.7%	100%	76%	14.7%	100%
Opuntia phaeacantha	80%	12.6%	100%	0%	0.0%	0%	0%	0.0%	0%
Yucca madrensis	0%	0.0%	0%	0%	0.0%	0%	0%	0.0%	0%
Tree									
Acacia constricta	88%	8.0%	100%	0%	0.0%	0%	0%	0.0%	0%
Acacia greggii	8%	8.0%	20%	76%	19.4%	80%	40%	14.1%	80%
Arbutus arizonica	0%	0.0%	0%	0%	0.0%	0%	0%	0.0%	0%
Arctostaphylos pringlei	0%	0.0%	0%	0%	0.0%	0%	0%	0.0%	0%
Celtis laevigata	0%	0.0%	0%	28%	19.6%	40%	4%	4.0%	20%
Celtis laevigata var. *reticulata*	0%	0.0%	0%	8%	8.0%	20%	4%	4.0%	20%
Chilopsis linearis	0%	0.0%	0%	0%	0.0%	0%	0%	0.0%	0%
Cupressus arizonica	0%	0.0%	0%	0%	0.0%	0%	0%	0.0%	0%
Dodonaea viscosa	0%	0.0%	0%	0%	0.0%	0%	20%	20.0%	20%
Erythrina flabelliformis	0%	0.0%	0%	0%	0.0%	0%	0%	0.0%	0%
Juniperus deppeana	0%	0.0%	0%	0%	0.0%	0%	0%	0.0%	0%
Parkinsonia microphylla	60%	16.7%	80%	48%	17.4%	80%	44%	20.4%	60%
Pinus arizonica	0%	0.0%	0%	0%	0.0%	0%	0%	0.0%	0%
Pinus discolor	4%	4.0%	20%	0%	0.0%	0%	0%	0.0%	0%
Pinus ponderosa	0%	0.0%	0%	0%	0.0%	0%	0%	0.0%	0%
Populus fremontii	0%	0.0%	0%	0%	0.0%	0%	0%	0.0%	0%
Prosopis glandulosa	0%	0.0%	0%	0%	0.0%	0%	0%	0.0%	0%
Prosopis velutina	56%	7.5%	100%	52%	19.6%	100%	68%	19.6%	100%

Table A4a. Within-plot and landscape frequency (%) for all plots and species sampled on monitoring plots, low-elevation strata, Rincon Mountain District, Saguaro NP, 2008–2010, cont.

Species	201 Within-plot Mean (%)	SE (%)	Stratum	202 Within-plot Mean (%)	SE (%)	Stratum	302 Within-plot Mean (%)	SE (%)	Stratum
Tree									
Pseudotsuga menziesii	0%	0.0%	0%	0%	0.0%	0%	0%	0.0%	0%
Quercus arizonica	0%	0.0%	0%	0%	0.0%	0%	0%	0.0%	0%
Quercus chrysolepis	0%	0.0%	0%	0%	0.0%	0%	0%	0.0%	0%
Quercus emoryi	0%	0.0%	0%	0%	0.0%	0%	0%	0.0%	0%
Quercus gambelii	0%	0.0%	0%	0%	0.0%	0%	0%	0.0%	0%
Quercus hypoleucoides	0%	0.0%	0%	0%	0.0%	0%	0%	0.0%	0%
Quercus oblongifolia	0%	0.0%	0%	0%	0.0%	0%	0%	0.0%	0%
Quercus rugosa	0%	0.0%	0%	0%	0.0%	0%	0%	0.0%	0%
Quercus toumeyi	0%	0.0%	0%	0%	0.0%	0%	0%	0.0%	0%
Quercus turbinella	0%	0.0%	0%	0%	0.0%	0%	0%	0.0%	0%
Rhamnus crocea	0%	0.0%	0%	0%	0.0%	0%	0%	0.0%	0%
Salix exigua	0%	0.0%	0%	20%	20.0%	20%	0%	0.0%	0%
Vauquelinia californica	0%	0.0%	0%	0%	0.0%	0%	0%	0.0%	0%
Vine									
Galactia wrightii	0%	0.0%	0%	0%	0.0%	0%	8%	8.0%	20%
Galium aparine	0%	0.0%	0%	0%	0.0%	0%	0%	0.0%	0%
Ipomoea barbatisepala	0%	0.0%	0%	0%	0.0%	0%	0%	0.0%	0%
Ipomoea coccinea	0%	0.0%	0%	0%	0.0%	0%	0%	0.0%	0%
Ipomoea tenuiloba	0%	0.0%	0%	0%	0.0%	0%	0%	0.0%	0%
Janusia gracilis	4%	4.0%	20%	68%	19.6%	100%	60%	16.7%	80%
Phaseolus	0%	0.0%	0%	0%	0.0%	0%	20%	12.6%	40%
Phaseolus ritensis	0%	0.0%	0%	0%	0.0%	0%	0%	0.0%	0%
Vicia	0%	0.0%	0%	0%	0.0%	0%	0%	0.0%	0%
Vicia pulchella	0%	0.0%	0%	0%	0.0%	0%	0%	0.0%	0%
Fern									
FERN	0%	0.0%	0%	8%	4.9%	40%	4%	4.0%	20%
Not identified to species									
Acourtia sp.	0%	0.0%	0%	0%	0.0%	0%	12%	8.0%	40%
Astrolepis sp.	0%	0.0%	0%	8%	8.0%	20%	8%	8.0%	20%
Calandrinia sp.	0%	0.0%	0%	0%	0.0%	0%	4%	4.0%	20%
Castilleja sp.	0%	0.0%	0%	0%	0.0%	0%	0%	0.0%	0%
Celtis sp.	0%	0.0%	0%	16%	16.0%	20%	8%	8.0%	20%
Cirsium sp.	0%	0.0%	0%	0%	0.0%	0%	8%	8.0%	20%
Cyperus sp.	0%	0.0%	0%	0%	0.0%	0%	0%	0.0%	0%
Draba sp.	0%	0.0%	0%	0%	0.0%	0%	0%	0.0%	0%
Dryopteris sp.	0%	0.0%	0%	0%	0.0%	0%	0%	0.0%	0%
Erigeron sp.	0%	0.0%	0%	0%	0.0%	0%	8%	8.0%	20%
Eriogonum sp.	0%	0.0%	0%	0%	0.0%	0%	16%	16.0%	20%
Galium sp.	0%	0.0%	0%	0%	0.0%	0%	0%	0.0%	0%
Hieracium sp.	0%	0.0%	0%	0%	0.0%	0%	0%	0.0%	0%
Lupinus sp.	0%	0.0%	0%	0%	0.0%	0%	0%	0.0%	0%
Notholaena sp.	0%	0.0%	0%	0%	0.0%	0%	4%	4.0%	20%
Penstemon sp.	0%	0.0%	0%	0%	0.0%	0%	4%	4.0%	20%

Table A4a. Within-plot and landscape frequency (%) for all plots and species sampled on monitoring plots, low-elevation strata, Rincon Mountain District, Saguaro NP, 2008–2010, cont.

Species	201 Within-plot			202 Within-plot			302 Within-plot		
	Mean (%)	SE (%)	Stratum	Mean (%)	SE (%)	Stratum	Mean (%)	SE (%)	Stratum
Not identified to species									
Trifolium sp.	0%	0.0%	0%	0%	0.0%	0%	0%	0.0%	0%
Verbena sp.	0%	0.0%	0%	0%	0.0%	0%	0%	0.0%	0%
Viola sp.	0%	0.0%	0%	0%	0.0%	0%	0%	0.0%	0%
Xanthisma sp.	0%	0.0%	0%	0%	0.0%	0%	8%	8.0%	20%

Table A4b. Within-plot and landscape frequency (%) for all plots and species sampled on monitoring plots, high-elevation and all strata, Rincon Mountain District, Saguaro NP, 2008–2010.

Species	402 Within-plot Mean (%)	SE (%)	Stratum	502 Within-plot Mean (%)	SE (%)	Stratum	All strata Within-plot Mean (%)	SE (%)	Landscape	MDC	n
Forb/Herb											
Acalypha sp.	0%	0.0%	0%	0%	0.0%	0%	1%	1%	3%	5%	0
Acourtia wrightii	3%	3.3%	8%	0%	0.0%	0%	2%	1%	5%	5%	8
Allionia incarnata	0%	0.0%	0%	0%	0.0%	0%	3%	2%	8%	5%	0
Amauriopsis dissecta	0%	0.0%	0%	2%	1.7%	8%	1%	1%	3%	5%	2
Ambrosia confertiflora	0%	0.0%	0%	0%	0.0%	0%	2%	2%	3%	5%	32
Antennaria marginata	0%	0.0%	0%	8%	8.3%	8%	3%	3%	3%	5%	49
Arenaria lanuginosa	0%	0.0%	0%	2%	1.7%	8%	1%	1%	3%	5%	2
Artemisia ludoviciana	17%	10.1%	23%	0%	0.0%	0%	9%	4%	18%	7%	54
Astrolepis cochisensis	8%	8.3%	8%	0%	0.0%	0%	3%	3%	3%	5%	49
Astrolepis sinuata	3%	2.2%	15%	5%	5.0%	8%	6%	3%	13%	5%	21
Bahia absinthifolia	0%	0.0%	0%	0%	0.0%	0%	3%	2%	8%	5%	25
Bidens leptocephala	2%	1.7%	8%	0%	0.0%	0%	1%	1%	3%	5%	2
Boerhavia sp.	3%	2.2%	15%	0%	0.0%	0%	1%	1%	5%	5%	4
Boerhavia coccinea	0%	0.0%	0%	3%	3.3%	8%	2%	1%	5%	5%	10
Bommeria hispida	12%	7.2%	31%	7%	6.7%	8%	6%	3%	10%	6%	47
Brickellia betonicifolia	3%	3.3%	8%	3%	3.3%	8%	2%	1%	5%	5%	16
Centaurea melitensis	0%	0.0%	0%	0%	0.0%	0%	1%	1%	3%	5%	2
Chamaesyce sp.	3%	2.2%	15%	0%	0.0%	0%	7%	3%	13%	6%	47
Cheilanthes sp.	33%	10.8%	46%	25%	10.2%	50%	22%	5%	38%	9%	56
Cheilanthes fendleri	13%	7.9%	23%	8%	8.3%	8%	7%	4%	10%	7%	48
Cheilanthes lindheimeri	5%	5.0%	8%	3%	3.3%	8%	3%	2%	5%	5%	25
Cheilanthes wootonii	2%	1.7%	8%	0%	0.0%	0%	1%	1%	3%	5%	2
Chenopodium	0%	0.0%	0%	0%	0.0%	0%	1%	1%	3%	5%	8
Cologania angustifolia	5%	5.0%	8%	0%	0.0%	0%	2%	2%	3%	5%	18
Cologania pallida	3%	3.3%	8%	0%	0.0%	0%	1%	1%	3%	5%	8
Commelina dianthifolia	0%	0.0%	0%	8%	5.8%	17%	3%	2%	5%	5%	25
Commelina erecta	7%	6.7%	8%	2%	1.7%	8%	3%	2%	5%	5%	33
Conyza bonariensis	0%	0.0%	0%	10%	5.2%	25%	3%	2%	8%	5%	23
Conyza canadensis	5%	5.0%	8%	7%	6.7%	8%	4%	2%	5%	5%	48
Dalea sp.	3%	2.2%	15%	0%	0.0%	0%	8%	4%	10%	5%	23
Daucus pusillus	0%	0.0%	0%	0%	0.0%	0%	1%	1%	3%	5%	0
Dieteria bigelovii	10%	7.2%	15%	0%	0.0%	0%	3%	2%	5%	5%	39
Draba helleriana	0%	0.0%	0%	10%	8.3%	17%	3%	3%	5%	5%	51
Drymaria leptophylla	0%	0.0%	0%	2%	1.7%	8%	1%	1%	3%	5%	2
Dryopteris filix-mas	0%	0.0%	0%	3%	2.2%	17%	1%	1%	5%	5%	4
Echeandia flavescens	0%	0.0%	0%	8%	6.7%	17%	3%	2%	5%	5%	33
Erigeron oreophilus	8%	8.3%	8%	33%	10.8%	50%	13%	5%	18%	9%	50
Eriogonum abertianum	3%	3.3%	8%	0%	0.0%	0%	1%	1%	3%	5%	8
Euphorbia heterophylla	0%	0.0%	0%	0%	0.0%	0%	1%	1%	3%	5%	2
Evolvulus alsinoides	0%	0.0%	0%	0%	0.0%	0%	1%	1%	0%	5%	2
Evolvulus arizonicus	7%	6.7%	8%	0%	0.0%	0%	3%	2%	3%	5%	39
Glandularia bipinnatifida	2%	1.7%	8%	2%	1.7%	8%	1%	1%	5%	5%	4
Gnaphalium sp.	0%	0.0%	0%	3%	3.3%	8%	2%	1%	5%	5%	8

Table A4b. Within-plot and landscape frequency (%) for all plots and species sampled on monitoring plots, high-elevation and all strata, Rincon Mountain District, Saguaro NP, 2008–2010, cont.

Species	402 Within-plot Mean (%)	SE (%)	Stratum	502 Within-plot Mean (%)	SE (%)	Stratum	All strata Within-plot Mean (%)	SE (%)	Landscape	MDC	n
Forb/Herb, cont.											
Hedeoma dentata	5%	5.0%	8%	0%	0.0%	0%	2%	2%	3%	5%	18
Hedeoma hyssopifolia	0%	0.0%	0%	2%	1.7%	8%	1%	1%	3%	5%	2
Hedeoma nana	2%	1.7%	8%	2%	1.7%	8%	1%	1%	5%	5%	4
Heterotheca sp.	2%	1.7%	8%	2%	1.7%	8%	1%	1%	5%	5%	4
Heuchera sp.	0%	0.0%	0%	2%	1.7%	8%	1%	1%	3%	5%	2
Heuchera sanguinea	3%	3.3%	8%	5%	5.0%	8%	3%	2%	5%	5%	25
Hymenothrix wrightii	0%	0.0%	0%	8%	8.3%	8%	3%	3%	3%	5%	49
Ipomoea sp.	8%	5.2%	23%	5%	3.6%	17%	7%	3%	18%	5%	29
Ipomoea ternifolia	0%	0.0%	0%	0%	0.0%	0%	3%	3%	3%	5%	0
Justicia longii	0%	0.0%	0%	0%	0.0%	0%	1%	1%	3%	5%	2
Koanophyllon	0%	0.0%	0%	0%	0.0%	0%	2%	2%	0%	5%	32
Linum neomexicanum	0%	0.0%	0%	3%	3.3%	8%	1%	1%	3%	5%	8
Lithospermum multiflorum	0%	0.0%	0%	3%	3.3%	8%	1%	1%	3%	5%	8
Lotus sp.	0%	0.0%	0%	3%	2.2%	17%	1%	1%	5%	5%	4
Machaeranthera	0%	0.0%	0%	0%	0.0%	0%	1%	1%	3%	5%	2
Machaeranthera tagetina	7%	6.7%	8%	0%	0.0%	0%	2%	2%	3%	5%	32
Macroptilium gibbosifolium	8%	5.8%	15%	7%	5.1%	17%	5%	2%	10%	5%	42
Malaxis soulei	0%	0.0%	0%	2%	1.7%	8%	1%	1%	3%	5%	2
Mentzelia sp.	2%	1.7%	8%	2%	1.7%	8%	1%	1%	5%	5%	4
Monarda citriodora ssp. austromontana	0%	0.0%	0%	2%	1.7%	8%	1%	1%	3%	5%	2
ANNUAL FORB	23%	9.5%	54%	27%	9.0%	58%	36%	5%	55%	10%	54
Nicotiana obtusifolia	0%	0.0%	0%	0%	0.0%	0%	1%	1%	3%	5%	2
Notholaena standleyi	7%	6.7%	8%	0%	0.0%	0%	5%	3%	5%	5%	52
Oxalis sp.	0%	0.0%	0%	8%	8.3%	8%	3%	3%	3%	5%	49
Packera neomexicana	7%	6.7%	8%	8%	5.8%	17%	5%	3%	8%	5%	54
Pellaea sp.	7%	5.1%	15%	0%	0.0%	0%	5%	3%	10%	5%	20
Pellaea truncata	13%	6.2%	38%	7%	5.1%	17%	9%	3%	23%	5%	59
Pellaea wrightiana	5%	2.6%	23%	0%	0.0%	0%	3%	1%	8%	5%	13
Penstemon barbatus	3%	3.3%	8%	0%	0.0%	0%	1%	1%	3%	5%	8
Pseudognaphalium canescens	13%	8.6%	23%	23%	11.2%	33%	12%	4%	20%	8%	58
Pseudognaphalium canescens ssp. canescens	13%	9.3%	23%	8%	6.7%	17%	7%	4%	10%	7%	48
Pseudognaphalium leucocephalum	0%	0.0%	0%	5%	5.0%	8%	2%	2%	3%	5%	18
Pteridium aquilinum	0%	0.0%	0%	7%	6.7%	8%	2%	2%	3%	5%	32
Salvia arizonica	0%	0.0%	0%	3%	2.2%	17%	2%	1%	8%	5%	4
Scrophularia parviflora	0%	0.0%	0%	7%	6.7%	8%	2%	2%	3%	5%	32
Sedum cockerellii	0%	0.0%	0%	3%	3.3%	8%	1%	1%	3%	5%	8
Selaginella arizonica	2%	1.7%	8%	0%	0.0%	0%	3%	2%	5%	5%	2
Selaginella rupincola	5%	5.0%	8%	0%	0.0%	0%	2%	2%	3%	5%	18
Solidago velutina	0%	0.0%	0%	2%	1.7%	8%	1%	1%	3%	5%	2

| | 402 | | | 502 | | | All strata | | | | |
| | Within-plot | | | Within-plot | | | Within-plot | | | | |
Species	Mean (%)	SE (%)	Stratum	Mean (%)	SE (%)	Stratum	Mean (%)	SE (%)	Landscape	MDC	n
Forb/Herb, cont.											
Stachys coccinea	3%	3.3%	8%	0%	0.0%	0%	1%	1%	3%	5%	8
Symphyotrichum	2%	1.7%	8%	0%	0.0%	0%	3%	2%	5%	5%	2
Thalictrum fendleri	0%	0.0%	0%	17%	9.5%	25%	5%	3%	8%	6%	49
Tradescantia pinetorum	0%	0.0%	0%	13%	9.3%	17%	4%	3%	5%	6%	45
Verbesina encelioides	8%	8.3%	8%	0%	0.0%	0%	3%	3%	3%	5%	49
Viola canadensis	0%	0.0%	0%	5%	3.6%	17%	2%	1%	5%	5%	10
Woodsia plummerae	0%	0.0%	0%	5%	5.0%	8%	2%	2%	3%	5%	18
Xanthisma gracile	3%	3.3%	8%	0%	0.0%	0%	1%	1%	3%	5%	8
Graminoid											
Aristida sp.	0%	0.0%	0%	0%	0.0%	0%	1%	1%	3%	5%	0
Aristida purpurea	28%	9.7%	46%	0%	0.0%	0%	17%	5%	30%	9%	53
Aristida schiedeana	25%	11.0%	38%	15%	8.9%	25%	17%	5%	28%	10%	54
Aristida ternipes	38%	9.7%	85%	3%	3.3%	8%	28%	5%	50%	8%	51
Aristida ternipes var. gentilis	0%	0.0%	0%	0%	0.0%	0%	2%	2%	0%	5%	18
Blepharoneuron tricholepis	0%	0.0%	0%	23%	9.8%	42%	7%	3%	13%	6%	60
Bothriochloa barbinodis	10%	4.6%	31%	0%	0.0%	0%	4%	2%	13%	5%	18
Bouteloua sp.	0%	0.0%	0%	0%	0.0%	0%	1%	1%	3%	5%	0
Bouteloua aristidoides	2%	1.7%	8%	0%	0.0%	0%	1%	1%	3%	5%	2
Bouteloua curtipendula	58%	10.6%	85%	13%	9.0%	17%	36%	7%	43%	10%	62
Bouteloua eriopoda	0%	0.0%	0%	0%	0.0%	0%	1%	1%	3%	5%	8
Bouteloua gracilis	3%	3.3%	8%	0%	0.0%	0%	1%	1%	3%	5%	8
Bouteloua hirsuta	17%	9.5%	31%	8%	8.3%	8%	8%	4%	13%	7%	58
Bouteloua repens	30%	11.1%	46%	8%	5.8%	17%	27%	6%	30%	10%	53
Bromus sp.	2%	1.7%	8%	8%	8.3%	8%	4%	3%	8%	5%	51
Bromus ciliatus	0%	0.0%	0%	12%	8.7%	17%	4%	3%	5%	5%	56
Bromus rubens	**8%**	**5.8%**	**15%**	**0%**	**0.0%**	**0%**	**6%**	**2%**	**13%**	**5%**	**32**
Carex geophila	0%	0.0%	0%	12%	8.0%	17%	4%	2%	5%	5%	48
Cenchrus ciliaris	**0%**	**0.0%**	**0%**	**0%**	**0.0%**	**0%**	**5%**	**3%**	**5%**	**5%**	**56**
Chloris virgata	3%	3.3%	8%	0%	0.0%	0%	1%	1%	3%	5%	8
Cyperus fendlerianus	2%	1.7%	8%	0%	0.0%	0%	1%	1%	3%	5%	2
Dasyochloa pulchella	2%	1.7%	8%	0%	0.0%	0%	5%	2%	13%	5%	34
Digitaria californica	3%	3.3%	8%	0%	0.0%	0%	15%	4%	23%	6%	60
Echinochloa sp.	**3%**	**3.3%**	**8%**	**0%**	**0.0%**	**0%**	**4%**	**2%**	**10%**	**5%**	**18**
Elymus sp.	0%	0.0%	0%	8%	8.3%	8%	3%	3%	3%	5%	49
Eragrostis sp.	2%	1.7%	8%	0%	0.0%	0%	1%	1%	3%	5%	2
Eragrostis cilianensis	**3%**	**3.3%**	**8%**	**0%**	**0.0%**	**0%**	**2%**	**1%**	**5%**	**5%**	**8**
Eragrostis intermedia	35%	8.6%	77%	20%	9.5%	33%	18%	5%	38%	9%	54
Eragrostis lehmanniana	**35%**	**11.6%**	**54%**	**0%**	**0.0%**	**0%**	**22%**	**6%**	**23%**	**10%**	**57**
Eriochloa lemmonii	3%	2.2%	15%	0%	0.0%	0%	1%	1%	5%	5%	4
Heteropogon contortus	17%	9.5%	23%	0%	0.0%	0%	11%	4%	18%	6%	50
Koeleria macrantha	0%	0.0%	0%	2%	1.7%	8%	1%	1%	3%	5%	2
Leptochloa dubia	20%	9.5%	31%	0%	0.0%	0%	6%	3%	10%	6%	53

Table A4b. Within-plot and landscape frequency (%) for all plots and species sampled on monitoring plots, high-elevation and all strata, Rincon Mountain District, Saguaro NP, 2008–2010, cont.

	402			502			All strata				
	Within-plot			Within-plot			Within-plot				
Species	Mean (%)	SE (%)	Stratum	Mean (%)	SE (%)	Stratum	Mean (%)	SE (%)	Landscape	MDC	n
Graminoid, cont.											
Muhlenbergia alopecuroides	47%	9.9%	85%	17%	10.1%	25%	19%	5%	33%	9%	62
Muhlenbergia emersleyi	88%	5.2%	100%	55%	12.8%	67%	46%	7%	53%	12%	60
Muhlenbergia polycaulis	2%	1.7%	8%	0%	0.0%	0%	2%	1%	5%	5%	2
Muhlenbergia porteri	0%	0.0%	0%	0%	0.0%	0%	28%	6%	25%	11%	55
ANNUAL GRASS	22%	6.7%	62%	8%	6.7%	17%	18%	4%	35%	8%	58
Panicum sp.	5%	3.6%	15%	0%	0.0%	0%	2%	1%	5%	5%	10
Panicum bulbosum	2%	1.7%	8%	2%	1.7%	8%	1%	1%	5%	5%	4
Panicum hirticaule	2%	1.7%	8%	0%	0.0%	0%	1%	1%	3%	5%	2
Piptochaetium fimbriatum	8%	5.2%	31%	10%	5.8%	25%	6%	2%	15%	5%	44
Piptochaetium pringlei	0%	0.0%	0%	5%	3.6%	17%	2%	1%	8%	5%	12
Poa fendleriana	2%	1.7%	8%	17%	11.2%	17%	6%	4%	8%	7%	49
Schizachyrium cirratum	12%	6.7%	23%	17%	9.2%	25%	9%	4%	18%	7%	48
Setaria sp.	0%	0.0%	0%	0%	0.0%	0%	1%	1%	3%	5%	0
Setaria grisebachii	3%	3.3%	8%	0%	0.0%	0%	2%	1%	3%	5%	16
Setaria leucopila	0%	0.0%	0%	0%	0.0%	0%	3%	3%	3%	5%	49
Sporobolus	0%	0.0%	0%	0%	0.0%	0%	2%	2%	3%	5%	0
Sporobolus wrightii	2%	1.7%	8%	0%	0.0%	0%	1%	1%	3%	5%	2
Trachypogon spicatus	12%	6.3%	23%	0%	0.0%	0%	4%	2%	8%	5%	32
Subshrub											
Abutilon sp.	0%	0.0%	0%	0%	0.0%	0%	3%	3%	3%	5%	2
Abutilon abutiloides	0%	0.0%	0%	0%	0.0%	0%	2%	2%	3%	5%	18
Abutilon incanum	0%	0.0%	0%	0%	0.0%	0%	9%	4%	8%	6%	64
Acacia angustissima	12%	8.7%	15%	0%	0.0%	0%	5%	3%	10%	5%	59
Adenophyllum porophylloides	0%	0.0%	0%	0%	0.0%	0%	1%	1%	3%	5%	2
Ageratina herbacea	2%	1.7%	8%	7%	5.1%	17%	3%	2%	8%	5%	21
Ambrosia ambrosioides	0%	0.0%	0%	0%	0.0%	0%	6%	3%	8%	5%	51
Ambrosia deltoidea	0%	0.0%	0%	0%	0.0%	0%	1%	1%	3%	5%	2
Ayenia filiformis	0%	0.0%	0%	0%	0.0%	0%	4%	3%	3%	5%	51
Baccharis brachyphylla	0%	0.0%	0%	0%	0.0%	0%	2%	1%	5%	5%	16
Bebbia juncea	0%	0.0%	0%	0%	0.0%	0%	3%	2%	8%	5%	28
Bouvardia ternifolia	0%	0.0%	0%	13%	9.3%	17%	4%	3%	5%	5%	65
Brickellia	7%	3.8%	31%	27%	10.8%	42%	13%	4%	25%	7%	58
Brickellia californica	18%	7.6%	46%	7%	3.8%	25%	8%	3%	23%	5%	58
Brickellia grandiflora	0%	0.0%	0%	25%	11.3%	33%	8%	4%	10%	7%	56
Brickellia simplex	0%	0.0%	0%	3%	3.3%	8%	1%	1%	3%	5%	8
Brickellia venosa	7%	6.7%	8%	0%	0.0%	0%	2%	2%	3%	5%	32
Comandra umbellata	5%	3.6%	15%	7%	5.1%	17%	4%	2%	10%	5%	28
Dalea albiflora	2%	1.7%	8%	5%	2.6%	25%	2%	1%	10%	5%	8
Dalea candida	0%	0.0%	0%	3%	3.3%	8%	1%	1%	3%	5%	8
Dalea lumholtzii	7%	6.7%	8%	0%	0.0%	0%	2%	2%	3%	5%	32
Dalea pulchra	0%	0.0%	0%	0%	0.0%	0%	2%	2%	0%	5%	32
Dalea versicolor	3%	3.3%	8%	0%	0.0%	0%	1%	1%	3%	5%	8

Table A4b. Within-plot and landscape frequency (%) for all plots and species sampled on monitoring plots, high-elevation and all strata, Rincon Mountain District, Saguaro NP, 2008–2010, cont.

Species	402 Within-plot Mean (%)	SE (%)	Stratum	502 Within-plot Mean (%)	SE (%)	Stratum	All strata Within-plot Mean (%)	SE (%)	Landscape	MDC	n
Subshrub, cont.											
Encelia farinosa	0%	0.0%	0%	0%	0.0%	0%	22%	6%	20%	10%	57
Ericameria laricifolia	20%	9.2%	38%	2%	1.7%	8%	18%	5%	28%	7%	50
Erigeron speciosus	0%	0.0%	0%	5%	5.0%	8%	2%	2%	3%	5%	18
Eriogonum wrightii	20%	9.2%	31%	7%	4.5%	17%	13%	4%	23%	7%	56
Galium stellatum	3%	3.3%	8%	0%	0.0%	0%	1%	1%	3%	5%	8
Galium wrightii	7%	6.7%	8%	0%	0.0%	0%	2%	2%	3%	5%	32
Geranium caespitosum	0%	0.0%	0%	5%	5.0%	8%	2%	2%	3%	5%	18
Gutierrezia sarothrae	2%	1.7%	8%	0%	0.0%	0%	1%	1%	3%	5%	2
Gymnosperma glutinosum	8%	8.3%	8%	0%	0.0%	0%	3%	3%	3%	5%	49
Hibiscus biseptus	0%	0.0%	0%	0%	0.0%	0%	3%	3%	3%	5%	49
Hibiscus coulteri	0%	0.0%	0%	0%	0.0%	0%	2%	2%	3%	5%	0
Ipomopsis multiflora	3%	2.2%	15%	13%	7.5%	25%	5%	2%	13%	5%	47
Isocoma tenuisecta	0%	0.0%	0%	0%	0.0%	0%	3%	2%	3%	5%	39
Lotus rigidus	0%	0.0%	0%	2%	1.7%	8%	1%	1%	3%	5%	2
Macrosiphonia brachysiphon	0%	0.0%	0%	0%	0.0%	0%	2%	2%	3%	5%	0
Manihot angustiloba	2%	1.7%	8%	0%	0.0%	0%	1%	1%	3%	5%	2
Menodora scabra	0%	0.0%	0%	0%	0.0%	0%	3%	3%	5%	5%	51
Nolina microcarpa	85%	7.0%	100%	37%	13.4%	42%	38%	7%	45%	13%	54
Penstemon linarioides	0%	0.0%	0%	5%	5.0%	8%	2%	2%	3%	5%	18
Perityle lemmonii	5%	5.0%	8%	0%	0.0%	0%	2%	2%	3%	5%	18
Phoradendron californicum	3%	3.3%	8%	0%	0.0%	0%	6%	3%	13%	5%	56
Phoradendron villosum	2%	1.7%	8%	0%	0.0%	0%	1%	1%	3%	5%	2
Porophyllum gracile	2%	1.7%	8%	0%	0.0%	0%	6%	3%	8%	6%	56
Psilostrophe cooperi	0%	0.0%	0%	0%	0.0%	0%	4%	2%	8%	5%	40
Rubus neomexicanus	0%	0.0%	0%	5%	5.0%	8%	2%	2%	3%	5%	18
Schoenocrambe linearifolia	7%	5.1%	15%	17%	9.2%	33%	7%	3%	15%	6%	57
Senna covesii	0%	0.0%	0%	0%	0.0%	0%	2%	1%	0%	5%	10
Sphaeralcea	7%	6.7%	8%	8%	5.8%	17%	8%	3%	15%	6%	48
Tagetes lemmonii	0%	0.0%	0%	2%	1.7%	8%	1%	1%	3%	5%	2
Talinum paniculatum	0%	0.0%	0%	0%	0.0%	0%	1%	1%	0%	5%	2
Tetramerium nervosum	0%	0.0%	0%	0%	0.0%	0%	1%	1%	3%	5%	2
Trichostema arizonicum	0%	0.0%	0%	7%	6.7%	8%	2%	2%	3%	5%	32
Trixis californica	0%	0.0%	0%	0%	0.0%	0%	7%	2%	8%	5%	29
Xanthisma spinulosum	0%	0.0%	0%	0%	0.0%	0%	2%	2%	3%	5%	18
Zinnia acerosa	0%	0.0%	0%	0%	0.0%	0%	9%	4%	13%	7%	52
Zinnia grandiflora	0%	0.0%	0%	0%	0.0%	0%	5%	3%	8%	6%	46
Shrub											
Aloysia wrightii	0%	0.0%	0%	0%	0.0%	0%	5%	2%	5%	5%	37
Amorpha californica	0%	0.0%	0%	3%	3.3%	8%	1%	1%	3%	5%	8
Anisacanthus thurberi	5%	5.0%	8%	0%	0.0%	0%	2%	2%	5%	5%	18
Arctostaphylos pungens	70%	10.3%	92%	50%	15.1%	50%	37%	7%	43%	13%	55

Table A4b. Within-plot and landscape frequency (%) for all plots and species sampled on monitoring plots, high-elevation and all strata, Rincon Mountain District, Saguaro NP, 2008–2010, cont.

	402			502			All strata				
	Within-plot			Within-plot			Within-plot				
Species	Mean (%)	SE (%)	Stratum	Mean (%)	SE (%)	Stratum	Mean (%)	SE (%)	Landscape	MDC	n
Shrub, cont.											
Baccharis	7%	4.5%	23%	0%	0.0%	0%	2%	1%	5%	5%	16
Baccharis sarothroides	5%	2.6%	23%	0%	0.0%	0%	2%	1%	8%	5%	6
Berberis wilcoxii	0%	0.0%	0%	2%	1.7%	8%	1%	1%	3%	5%	2
Calliandra sp.	0%	0.0%	0%	0%	0.0%	0%	6%	4%	5%	5%	56
Calliandra eriophylla	2%	1.7%	8%	0%	0.0%	0%	13%	5%	13%	7%	63
Calliandra humilis	0%	0.0%	0%	8%	6.7%	17%	5%	3%	8%	6%	59
Ceanothus fendleri	7%	6.7%	8%	12%	6.3%	25%	6%	3%	10%	5%	60
Ceanothus greggii	0%	0.0%	0%	3%	3.3%	8%	1%	1%	3%	5%	8
Ceanothus integerrimus	0%	0.0%	0%	5%	5.0%	8%	2%	2%	3%	5%	18
Celtis ehrenbergiana	0%	0.0%	0%	0%	0.0%	0%	3%	2%	8%	5%	6
Condalia	3%	3.3%	8%	0%	0.0%	0%	7%	3%	10%	6%	58
Condalia correllii	7%	6.7%	8%	0%	0.0%	0%	2%	2%	3%	5%	32
Condalia warnockii	0%	0.0%	0%	0%	0.0%	0%	2%	1%	5%	5%	10
Coursetia glandulosa	0%	0.0%	0%	0%	0.0%	0%	2%	2%	0%	5%	18
Crossosoma bigelovii	0%	0.0%	0%	0%	0.0%	0%	4%	3%	8%	5%	2
Ephedra sp.	0%	0.0%	0%	0%	0.0%	0%	1%	1%	5%	5%	4
Ephedra trifurca	0%	0.0%	0%	0%	0.0%	0%	4%	3%	5%	5%	56
Eriodictyon angustifolium	2%	1.7%	8%	0%	0.0%	0%	1%	1%	3%	5%	2
Fendlera rupicola	5%	5.0%	8%	0%	0.0%	0%	2%	2%	3%	5%	18
Fouquieria splendens	10%	4.6%	31%	0%	0.0%	0%	18%	5%	20%	8%	58
Frangula californica	0%	0.0%	0%	2%	1.7%	8%	1%	1%	3%	5%	2
Garrya wrightii	37%	11.0%	62%	35%	11.0%	58%	22%	5%	35%	10%	53
Gossypium thurberi	12%	8.7%	15%	0%	0.0%	0%	9%	4%	13%	5%	62
Holodiscus discolor	0%	0.0%	0%	3%	3.3%	8%	1%	1%	3%	5%	8
Holodiscus dumosus	0%	0.0%	0%	3%	3.3%	8%	1%	1%	3%	5%	8
Jacquemontia pringlei	0%	0.0%	0%	0%	0.0%	0%	1%	1%	0%	5%	8
Jatropha cardiophylla	0%	0.0%	0%	0%	0.0%	0%	15%	5%	10%	8%	59
Larrea tridentata	0%	0.0%	0%	0%	0.0%	0%	9%	4%	10%	8%	56
Lycium	0%	0.0%	0%	0%	0.0%	0%	3%	1%	5%	5%	12
Lycium andersonii	0%	0.0%	0%	0%	0.0%	0%	6%	3%	3%	7%	52
Lycium berlandieri	0%	0.0%	0%	0%	0.0%	0%	1%	1%	3%	5%	8
Lycium pallidum	0%	0.0%	0%	0%	0.0%	0%	2%	2%	0%	5%	32
Matelea parvifolia	0%	0.0%	0%	0%	0.0%	0%	1%	1%	3%	5%	2
Mimosa aculeaticarpa	22%	9.0%	38%	10%	8.3%	17%	10%	4%	18%	7%	59
Mimosa aculeaticarpa var. *biuncifera*	7%	6.7%	15%	0%	0.0%	0%	3%	2%	5%	5%	39
SNAG	82%	4.6%	100%	90%	3.9%	100%	87%	2%	85%	7%	60
Plumbago zeylanica	0%	0.0%	0%	0%	0.0%	0%	1%	1%	3%	5%	8
Rhus aromatica	2%	1.7%	8%	0%	0.0%	0%	1%	1%	3%	5%	2
Robinia neomexicana	0%	0.0%	0%	10%	7.2%	17%	3%	2%	5%	5%	39
Symphoricarpos	0%	0.0%	0%	3%	2.2%	17%	1%	1%	5%	5%	4
Symphoricarpos oreophilus	0%	0.0%	0%	5%	5.0%	8%	2%	2%	3%	5%	18
Ziziphus obtusifolia	0%	0.0%	0%	0%	0.0%	0%	5%	2%	8%	5%	27

Species	402 Within-plot Mean (%)	SE (%)	Stratum	502 Within-plot Mean (%)	SE (%)	Stratum	All strata Within-plot Mean (%)	SE (%)	Landscape	MDC	n
Succulent											
Agave palmeri	27%	8.6%	62%	18%	10.3%	25%	22%	5%	35%	8%	57
Agave parryi	3%	2.2%	15%	0%	0.0%	0%	1%	1%	5%	5%	4
Agave schottii	53%	11.4%	85%	12%	8.7%	17%	23%	6%	33%	10%	57
Carnegiea gigantea	0%	0.0%	0%	0%	0.0%	0%	14%	4%	18%	8%	62
Cylindropuntia sp.	0%	0.0%	0%	0%	0.0%	0%	4%	3%	0%	5%	65
Cylindropuntia acanthocarpa	0%	0.0%	0%	0%	0.0%	0%	5%	3%	8%	5%	34
Cylindropuntia arbuscula	0%	0.0%	0%	0%	0.0%	0%	1%	1%	5%	5%	4
Cylindropuntia bigelovii	0%	0.0%	0%	0%	0.0%	0%	4%	3%	0%	5%	56
Cylindropuntia fulgida	0%	0.0%	0%	0%	0.0%	0%	4%	3%	5%	5%	65
Cylindropuntia fulgida var. mamillata	0%	0.0%	0%	0%	0.0%	0%	1%	1%	3%	5%	2
Cylindropuntia leptocaulis	0%	0.0%	0%	0%	0.0%	0%	7%	3%	10%	6%	54
Cylindropuntia spinosior	13%	6.2%	38%	10%	7.2%	17%	8%	3%	15%	6%	46
Cylindropuntia versicolor	2%	1.7%	8%	0%	0.0%	0%	17%	5%	18%	9%	53
Dasylirion wheeleri	37%	11.0%	62%	7%	6.7%	8%	18%	5%	30%	8%	60
Echinocereus sp.	2%	1.7%	8%	7%	5.1%	17%	4%	2%	10%	5%	28
Echinocereus fendleri	0%	0.0%	0%	2%	1.7%	8%	3%	2%	8%	5%	27
Echinocereus pectinatus	3%	3.3%	8%	0%	0.0%	0%	1%	1%	3%	5%	8
Echinocereus rigidissimus	2%	1.7%	8%	0%	0.0%	0%	1%	1%	3%	5%	2
Echinocereus triglochidiatus	0%	0.0%	0%	2%	1.7%	8%	1%	1%	3%	5%	2
Escobaria vivipara	2%	1.7%	8%	0%	0.0%	0%	1%	1%	3%	5%	2
Ferocactus wislizeni	10%	5.8%	31%	0%	0.0%	0%	27%	5%	30%	9%	60
Mammillaria	8%	5.2%	23%	0%	0.0%	0%	16%	5%	18%	8%	57
Mammillaria grahamii	3%	2.2%	15%	3%	3.3%	8%	10%	4%	20%	6%	49
Opuntia	5%	5.0%	8%	0%	0.0%	0%	3%	2%	5%	5%	21
Opuntia chlorotica	2%	1.7%	8%	3%	3.3%	8%	2%	1%	5%	5%	10
Opuntia engelmannii	22%	9.0%	46%	3%	3.3%	8%	33%	6%	38%	10%	59
Opuntia phaeacantha	0%	0.0%	0%	3%	3.3%	8%	11%	5%	15%	8%	62
Yucca madrensis	40%	10.7%	77%	48%	12.4%	67%	27%	6%	43%	10%	64
Tree											
Acacia constricta	0%	0.0%	0%	0%	0.0%	0%	11%	5%	13%	9%	54
Acacia greggii	5%	5.0%	8%	0%	0.0%	0%	17%	5%	15%	9%	54
Arbutus arizonica	0%	0.0%	0%	5%	3.6%	17%	2%	1%	5%	5%	10
Arctostaphylos pringlei	8%	8.3%	8%	3%	3.3%	8%	4%	3%	5%	5%	56
Celtis laevigata	0%	0.0%	0%	0%	0.0%	0%	4%	3%	3%	5%	56
Celtis laevigata var. reticulata	0%	0.0%	0%	0%	0.0%	0%	2%	1%	3%	5%	10
Chilopsis linearis	2%	1.7%	8%	0%	0.0%	0%	1%	1%	3%	5%	2
Cupressus arizonica	0%	0.0%	0%	2%	1.7%	8%	1%	1%	3%	5%	2
Dodonaea viscosa	0%	0.0%	0%	0%	0.0%	0%	3%	3%	3%	5%	0
Erythrina flabelliformis	2%	1.7%	8%	0%	0.0%	0%	1%	1%	3%	5%	2
Juniperus deppeana	17%	7.3%	46%	47%	11.9%	67%	19%	5%	33%	10%	49

Table A4b. Within-plot and landscape frequency (%) for all plots and species sampled on monitoring plots, high-elevation and all strata, Rincon Mountain District, Saguaro NP, 2008–2010, cont.

	402			502			All strata				
	Within-plot			Within-plot			Within-plot				
Species	Mean (%)	SE (%)	Stratum	Mean (%)	SE (%)	Stratum	Mean (%)	SE (%)	Landscape	MDC	n
Tree, cont.											
Parkinsonia microphylla	0%	0.0%	0%	0%	0.0%	0%	19%	5%	18%	10%	58
Pinus arizonica	0%	0.0%	0%	8%	6.7%	17%	3%	2%	5%	5%	33
Pinus discolor	23%	11.5%	38%	45%	12.1%	67%	22%	6%	33%	10%	60
Pinus ponderosa	0%	0.0%	0%	30%	12.2%	42%	9%	4%	13%	8%	53
Populus fremontii	2%	1.7%	8%	0%	0.0%	0%	1%	1%	3%	5%	2
Prosopis glandulosa	3%	3.3%	8%	0%	0.0%	0%	1%	1%	3%	5%	8
Prosopis velutina	10%	7.2%	15%	0%	0.0%	0%	26%	6%	30%	9%	52
Pseudotsuga menziesii	0%	0.0%	0%	20%	10.7%	25%	6%	3%	8%	6%	64
Quercus arizonica	35%	10.8%	62%	30%	10.6%	50%	20%	5%	33%	9%	60
Quercus chrysolepis	0%	0.0%	0%	2%	1.7%	8%	1%	1%	3%	5%	2
Quercus emoryi	57%	9.8%	85%	15%	10.2%	17%	22%	6%	30%	10%	59
Quercus gambelii	0%	0.0%	0%	13%	8.6%	25%	4%	3%	8%	5%	57
Quercus hypoleucoides	10%	8.3%	15%	48%	13.1%	67%	18%	6%	25%	10%	60
Quercus oblongifolia	7%	3.8%	23%	0%	0.0%	0%	2%	1%	8%	5%	12
Quercus rugosa	0%	0.0%	0%	45%	12.6%	67%	14%	5%	20%	9%	58
Quercus toumeyi	3%	3.3%	8%	0%	0.0%	0%	1%	1%	3%	5%	8
Quercus turbinella	0%	0.0%	0%	3%	3.3%	8%	1%	1%	3%	5%	8
Rhamnus crocea	2%	1.7%	8%	0%	0.0%	0%	1%	1%	3%	5%	2
Salix exigua	0%	0.0%	0%	0%	0.0%	0%	3%	3%	0%	5%	49
Vauquelinia californica	2%	1.7%	8%	0%	0.0%	0%	1%	1%	3%	5%	2
Vine											
Galactia wrightii	0%	0.0%	0%	0%	0.0%	0%	1%	1%	3%	5%	0
Galium aparine	0%	0.0%	0%	3%	3.3%	8%	1%	1%	3%	5%	8
Ipomoea barbatisepala	7%	6.7%	8%	0%	0.0%	0%	2%	2%	3%	5%	32
Ipomoea coccinea	13%	8.6%	23%	2%	1.7%	8%	5%	3%	10%	5%	58
Ipomoea tenuiloba	2%	1.7%	8%	3%	2.2%	17%	2%	1%	8%	5%	6
Janusia gracilis	0%	0.0%	0%	0%	0.0%	0%	17%	5%	13%	9%	61
Phaseolus	8%	8.3%	8%	5%	3.6%	17%	7%	3%	13%	5%	57
Phaseolus ritensis	2%	1.7%	8%	7%	6.7%	8%	3%	2%	5%	5%	33
Vicia	0%	0.0%	0%	5%	5.0%	8%	2%	2%	3%	5%	18
Vicia pulchella	0%	0.0%	0%	5%	3.6%	17%	2%	1%	5%	5%	10
Fern											
FERN	12%	8.3%	23%	0%	0.0%	0%	5%	3%	10%	5%	55
Not identified to species											
Acourtia sp.	0%	0.0%	0%	0%	0.0%	0%	2%	1%	5%	5%	8
Astrolepis sp.	7%	5.1%	15%	3%	3.3%	8%	5%	2%	10%	5%	43
Calandrinia sp.	0%	0.0%	0%	0%	0.0%	0%	1%	1%	3%	5%	0
Castilleja sp.	2%	1.7%	8%	3%	3.3%	8%	2%	1%	5%	5%	10
Celtis sp.	0%	0.0%	0%	0%	0.0%	0%	3%	2%	3%	5%	40
Cirsium sp.	3%	2.2%	15%	0%	0.0%	0%	2%	1%	8%	5%	4
Cyperus sp.	5%	2.6%	31%	8%	3.9%	33%	4%	2%	18%	5%	17
Draba sp.	0%	0.0%	0%	2%	1.7%	8%	1%	1%	3%	5%	2
Dryopteris sp.	0%	0.0%	0%	2%	1.7%	8%	1%	1%	3%	5%	2

Table A4b. Within-plot and landscape frequency (%) for all plots and species sampled on monitoring plots, high-elevation and all strata, Rincon Mountain District, Saguaro NP, 2008–2010, cont.

Species	402 Within-plot Mean (%)	SE (%)	Stratum	502 Within-plot Mean (%)	SE (%)	Stratum	All strata Within-plot Mean (%)	SE (%)	Landscape	MDC	n
Not identified to species, cont.											
Erigeron sp.	3%	2.2%	15%	7%	6.7%	8%	4%	2%	10%	5%	35
Eriogonum sp.	5%	3.6%	15%	2%	1.7%	8%	4%	2%	10%	5%	12
Galium sp.	0%	0.0%	0%	18%	11.1%	25%	6%	4%	8%	7%	49
Hieracium sp.	0%	0.0%	0%	2%	1.7%	8%	1%	1%	3%	5%	2
Lupinus sp.	0%	0.0%	0%	2%	1.7%	8%	1%	1%	3%	5%	2
Notholaena sp.	0%	0.0%	0%	0%	0.0%	0%	1%	1%	3%	5%	0
Penstemon sp.	0%	0.0%	0%	0%	0.0%	0%	1%	1%	3%	5%	2
Trifolium sp.	0%	0.0%	0%	2%	1.7%	8%	1%	1%	3%	5%	2
Verbena sp.	3%	3.3%	8%	0%	0.0%	0%	1%	1%	3%	5%	8
Viola sp.	0%	0.0%	0%	2%	1.7%	8%	1%	1%	3%	5%	2
Xanthisma sp.	8%	8.3%	8%	0%	0.0%	0%	4%	3%	5%	5%	49

Table A5a. Soil substrate (% by class) and surface aggregate stability class (mean and SE) and proportion of samples in "very stable" (=6) category, low-elevation strata, Rincon Mountain District, Saguaro NP, 2008–2010.

Parameter	201				202				302			
	AVG	SE	MDC	n=	AVG	SE	MDC	n=	AVG	SE	MDC	n=
Substrate												
Bare soil (<2 mm), no overhead cover	8.1%	0.8%	5%	1	5.4%	1.7%	5%	3	2.7%	1.2%	5%	2
Bare soil (<2 mm), under vegetation	7.6%	1.5%	5%	2	7.8%	2.9%	5%	8	7.0%	1.6%	5%	3
Light cyanobacteria, no overhead cover	3.4%	1.3%	5%	2	0.3%	0.3%	5%	1	0.0%	0.0%	5%	0
Light cyanobacteria, under vegetation	1.9%	0.8%	5%	1	0.2%	0.2%	5%	1	0.2%	0.1%	5%	1
Litter and duff (organic matter)	26.9%	2.3%	5%	5	26.4%	8.9%	13%	11	35.8%	5.4%	9%	8
Dark cyanobacteria	0.9%	0.7%	5%	1	0.3%	0.2%	5%	1	0.0%	0.0%	5%	0
Gravel (2–75 mm)	44.4%	1.8%	5%	3	33.8%	9.0%	13%	11	19.4%	5.3%	9%	8
Lichen	1.6%	1.0%	5%	1	0.3%	0.2%	5%	1	0.2%	0.1%	5%	1
Moss	0.1%	0.1%	5%	1	5.3%	3.1%	5%	9	2.3%	2.0%	5%	4
Rock (76–600 mm)	0.9%	0.4%	5%	1	6.2%	1.9%	5%	4	11.2%	3.8%	7%	7
Plant base	3.3%	0.6%	5%	1	3.1%	0.7%	5%	1	3.2%	0.8%	5%	1
Bedrock	0.8%	0.8%	5%	1	10.7%	3.8%	6%	9	18.3%	5.2%	9%	8
Surface Soil Aggregate Stability												
Under cover												
Average soil stability	4.62	0.23	0.5	5	4.02	0.42	0.6	11	4.34	0.40	0.7	8
% samples "very stable"	41%	4%	8%	5	34%	8%	11%	11	42%	9%	16%	8
Not under cover												
Average soil stability	3.79	0.27	0.6	5	3.24	0.63	0.9	11	3.45	0.43	0.7	8
% samples "very stable"	25%	10%	20%	5	25%	12%	17%	11	28%	11%	18%	8

Decreasing erosion hazard ↓

Table A5b. Soil substrate (% by class) and surface aggregate stability class (mean and SE) and proportion of samples in "very stable" (=6) category, high-elevation and all strata, Rincon Mountain District, Saguaro NP, 2008–2010.

Parameter	402 AVG	402 SE	402 MDC	402 n=	502 AVG	502 SE	502 MDC	502 n=	Parkwide AVG	Parkwide SE	Parkwide MDC	Parkwide n=
Substrate												
Bare soil (<2 mm), no overhead cover	2.5%	0.5%	5%	1	1.6%	0.6%	5%	1	3.3%	0.5%	5%	2
Bare soil (<2 mm), under vegetation	3.8%	0.7%	5%	1	3.8%	0.9%	5%	2	5.2%	0.6%	5%	3
Light cyanobacteria, no overhead cover	0.0%	0.0%	5%	1	0.1%	0.1%	5%	1	0.3%	0.1%	5%	1
Light cyanobacteria, under vegetation	0.0%	0.0%	5%	1	0.0%	0.0%	5%	0	0.5%	0.2%	5%	1
Litter and duff (organic matter)	42.0%	4.0%	7%	17	66.7%	4.1%	7%	18	44.9%	3.3%	6%	51
Dark cyanobacteria	0.03%	0.0%	5%	1	0.0%	0.0%	5%	0	0.2%	0.1%	5%	1
Gravel (2–75 mm)	25.6%	4.4%	8%	16	15.2%	2.4%	5%	12	25.1%	2.5%	5%	41
Lichen	0.0%	0.0%	5%	1	0.5%	0.3%	5%	1	0.4%	0.2%	5%	1
Moss	0.9%	0.6%	5%	1	0.4%	0.1%	5%	1	1.4%	0.5%	5%	2
Rock (76–600 mm)	4.9%	1.1%	5%	3	5.3%	0.9%	5%	2	5.5%	0.8%	5%	5
Plant base	6.3%	1.1%	5%	3	3.1%	1.4%	5%	5	4.1%	0.6%	5%	3
Bedrock	13.9%	4.0%	7%	18	3.3%	1.3%	5%	4	9.1%	1.8%	5%	21
Surface Soil Aggregate Stability												
Under cover												
Average soil stability	4.23	0.24	0.40	18	4.16	0.32	0.60	14	4.25	0.14	0.30	35
% samples "very stable"	41.5%	4.3%	7%	20	43.8%	6.2%	10%	18	41.4%	2.65%	5%	47
Not under cover												
Average soil stability	3.77	0.33	0.60	18	3.04	0.43	0.80	14	3.45	0.23	0.40	39
% samples "very stable"	25.3%	6.7%	11%	20	20.1%	7.0%	12%	17	24.1%	3.59%	6%	60

Decreasing erosion hazard

Table A6a. Biological soil crust cover (% by class), as measured by point-quadrats, low-elevation strata, Rincon Mountain District, Saguaro NP, 2008–2010.

Lichen growth form / morphological group	201				202				302			
	AVG	SE	MDC	n=	AVG	SE	MDC	n=	AVG	SE	MDC	n=
Crustose lichen	0.0%	0.0%	5%	1	0.0%	0.0%	5%	1	0.2%	0.2%	5%	1
Gelatinous lichen	0.0%	0.0%	5%	1	0.0%	0.0%	5%	1	0.0%	0.0%	5%	1
Folise lichen	0.0%	0.0%	5%	1	0.0%	0.0%	5%	1	0.0%	0.0%	5%	1
Fruticose lichen	0.0%	0.0%	5%	1	0.0%	0.0%	5%	1	0.0%	0.0%	5%	1
Squamulose lichen	0.0%	0.0%	5%	1	0.2%	0.2%	5%	1	0.7%	0.7%	5%	1
Unknown lichen	0.4%	0.4%	5%	1	0.0%	0.0%	5%	1	0.0%	0.0%	5%	1
Lichen-dominated soil crust (total)	*0.4%*	*0.4%*	*5%*	*1*	*0.2%*	*0.2%*	*5%*	*1*	*0.9%*	*0.9%*	*5%*	*1*
Light cyanobacteria soil crust	12.2%	6.3%	9%	5	0.3%	0.3%	5%	1	0.5%	0.5%	5%	1
Dark cyanobacteria soil crust	2.5%	2.1%	5%	2	0.2%	0.2%	5%	1	0.0%	0.0%	5%	1
Bryophyte dominated soil crust	0.0%	0.0%	5%	1	4.8%	2.2%	5%	2	3.6%	3.6%	5%	5
Dark cyanobacteria, lichen, or bryophyte	*2.8%*	*2.5%*	*5%*	*3*	*5.1%*	*2.2%*	*5%*	*2*	*4.5%*	*4.5%*	*9%*	*3*

Table A6b. Biological soil crust cover (% by class), as measured by point-quadrats, high-elevation and all strata, Rincon Mountain District, Saguaro NP, 2008–2010.

Lichen growth form / morphological group	402				502				Parkwide			
	AVG	SE	MDC	n=	AVG	SE	MDC	n=	AVG	SE	MDC	n=
Crustose lichen	0.0%	0.0%	5%	1	0.0%	0.0%	5%	1	0.03%	0.03%	5%	1
Gelatinous lichen	0.0%	0.0%	5%	1	0.0%	0.0%	5%	1	0.0%	0.0%	5%	1
Folise lichen	0.0%	0.0%	5%	1	0.0%	0.0%	5%	1	0.0%	0.0%	5%	1
Fruticose lichen	0.0%	0.0%	5%	1	0.0%	0.0%	5%	1	0.0%	0.0%	5%	1
Squamulose lichen	0.4%	0.4%	5%	1	0.5%	0.5%	5%	1	0.4%	0.21%	6%	1
Unknown lichen	0.0%	0.0%	5%	1	0.0%	0.0%	5%	1	0.1%	0.1%	5%	1
Lichen dominated soil crust (total)	*0.4%*	*0.4%*	*5%*	*1*	*0.5%*	*0.5%*	*5%*	*1*	*0.5%*	*0.2%*	*5%*	*1*
Light cyanobacteria soil crust	3.3%	1.5%	5%	2	4.5%	2.8%	5%	3	4.0%	1.6%	5%	5
Dark cyanobacteria soil crust	0.3%	0.3%	5%	1	0.3%	0.0%	5%	1	0.6%	0.4%	5%	1
Bryophyte dominated soil crust	1.1%	0.4%	5%	1	0.0%	0.0%	5%	1	1.7%	0.8%	5%	2
Dark cyanobacteria, lichen, or bryophyte	*1.9%*	*0.8%*	*5%*	*1*	*0.9%*	*0.5%*	*5%*	*1*	*2.8%*	*0.9%*	*5%*	*2*

Table A7a. Within-plot and landscape frequency (%) for biological soil crust morphological groups and lichen growth forms sampled on monitoring plots, low-elevation strata, Rincon Mountain District, Saguaro NP, 2008–2010.

Lichen growth form / morphological group	201			202			302		
	Within-plot			Within-plot			Within-plot		
	Mean (%)	SE (%)	Stratum	Mean (%)	SE (%)	Stratum	Mean (%)	SE (%)	Stratum
Crustose lichen	7%	5.3%	50%	6%	5.6%	50%	8%	8.3%	50%
Gelatinous lichen	0%	0.0%	0%	0%	0.0%	0%	0%	0.0%	0%
Folise lichen	0%	0.0%	0%	0%	0.0%	0%	0%	0.0%	0%
Fruticose lichen	0%	0.0%	0%	0%	0.0%	0%	0%	0.0%	0%
Squamulose lichen	7%	5.3%	50%	14%	8.3%	100%	8%	8.3%	50%
Unknown lichen	10%	9.7%	25%	0%	0.0%	0%	0%	0.0%	0%
Lichen dominated soil crust (total)	*19%*	*8.6%*	*75%*	*14%*	*8.3%*	*100%*	*14%*	*13.9%*	*50%*
Light cyanobacteria soil crust	86%	2.8%	100%	22%	16.7%	100%	3%	2.8%	50%
Dark cyanobacteria soil crust	38%	4.2%	100%	17%	0.0%	100%	0%	0.0%	0%
Bryophyte dominated soil crust	3%	2.8%	25%	44%	5.6%	100%	36%	36.1%	50%
Dark cyanobacteria, lichen, or bryophyte	*40%*	*6.2%*	*100%*	*58%*	*2.8%*	*100%*	*39%*	*38.9%*	*50%*

Table A7b. Within-plot and landscape frequency (%) for biological soil crust morphological groups and lichen growth forms sampled on monitoring plots at the Rincon Mountain District, Saguaro NP, 2008–2010.

Lichen growth form / morphological group	402			502			All strata				
	Within-plot			Within-plot			Within-plot				
	Mean (%)	SE (%)	Stratum	Mean (%)	SE (%)	Stratum	Mean (%)	SE (%)	Landscape	MDC	n
Crustose lichen	0%	0.0%	0%	0%	0.0%	0%	4%	2%	20%	5%	9
Gelatinous lichen	4%	2.7%	40%	6%	5.6%	50%	2%	1%	20%	3%	4
Folise lichen	0%	0.0%	0%	0%	0.0%	0%	0%	0%	0%	0%	0
Fruticose lichen	0%	0.0%	0%	0%	0.0%	0%	0%	0%	0%	0%	0
Squamulose lichen	2%	2.2%	20%	14%	13.9%	50%	7%	3%	33%	7%	18
Unknown lichen	0%	0.0%	0%	0%	0.0%	0%	3%	3%	7%	7%	18
Lichen dominated soil crust (total)	*6%*	*3.5%*	*40%*	*19%*	*8.3%*	*100%*	*13%*	*3%*	*53%*	*9%*	*15*
Light cyanobacteria soil crust	43%	16.1%	80%	61%	22.2%	100%	49%	9%	73%	26%	57
Dark cyanobacteria soil crust	17%	7.7%	80%	19%	19.4%	50%	20%	4%	60%	12%	52
Bryophyte dominated soil crust	34%	10.2%	100%	39%	5.6%	100%	28%	6%	60%	17%	54
Dark cyanobacteria, lichen, or bryophyte	*42%*	*10.3%*	*100%*	*44%*	*0.0%*	*100%*	*44%*	*5%*	*80%*	*15%*	*53*

www.ingramcontent.com/pod-product-compliance
Lightning Source LLC
Chambersburg PA
CBHW081140290526
45795CB00006B/2309